Copyright © MCMLXXI by Fred Powell
All rights reserved.
This 1979 edition is published by Bonanza Books,
distributed by Crown Publishers, Inc.,
by arrangement with Educator Books, Inc.

Manufactured in the United States of America

Library of Congress Cataloging in Publication Data

Powell, Fred.
    The bartender's standard manual.

    1. Cocktails. I. Title.
TX951.P58   1979   641.8'74   79-9184
ISBN 0-517-293056

p o n

INTRODUCTION

The science of skillfully mixing drinks is the subject of several worthwhile books. *The Bartender's Standard Manual* represents an effort to provide the professional with a standard listing of drink recipes in a concise quick-reference form.

There are over 700 standard recipes listed in continuous alphabetical order. Easily readable type is used to help overcome subdued lighting often found in actual working conditions. Wording is minimized with little comment on "technique."

The compiling and editing of these chosen recipes is a giant step forward in *standardizing* the quality of mixed drinks. This achievement, which has been long in its evolution, is most desirable because Standard Quality gracefully serves both host and guest.

It would be an achievement, indeed, for each martini in New York City to be equally perfect . . . and, for them to be identical with all other martinis served in San Francisco, New Orleans, Chicago, Houston, and throughout the entire United States. That is the goal . . . because America is a traveling nation of individuals who insist upon quality. Your part in making a national standard of quality in mixing drinks is easy . . . simply use this convenient reference book.

Special Section Of Party Punches
And Nogs Starts On Page 95

ABBEY STANDARD

1 jigger gin
¾ ounce orange juice
1 dash orange bitters

Shake with cracked ice and strain. Garnish with maraschino cherry.

ADDINGTON

1 jigger Sweet Vermouth
1 jigger Dry Vermouth

Stir with ice and strain. Fill with Soda Water and serve with twist of Lemon Peel.

ADONIS

1 jigger Dry Sherry
½ jigger Sweet Vermouth
1 Dash Orange Bitters

Stir with ice. Strain.

AFFINITY

1 jigger Scotch Whisky
1 jigger Dry Vermouth
1 jigger Sweet Vermouth
2 Dashes Angostura Bitters

Stir with ice and strain. Serve with a Cherry and twist a Lemon Peel over top of glass.

AFFINITY COCKTAIL

1 jigger Scotch
½ jigger Dry Vermouth
½ jigger Sweet Vermouth
2 Dashes Bitters

Stir with ice. Strain. Serve with c h e r r y and twist of lemon peel.

AFTER SUPPER

1 jigger Apricot Brandy
1 jigger Curacao
2 Dashes Lemon Juice

Stir with ice and strain.

AFTER-DINNER

1 jigger Swedish Punch
½ jigger Cherry Brandy
Juice of ½ Lime

Shake with ice and strain.

ALASKA

1 jigger Dry Gin
½ jigger Yellow Chartreuse
2 Dashes Orange Bitters

Stir with ice and strain. Serve with a twist of Lemon Peel.

1

ALBEMARLE

2 jiggers Dry Gin
½ Tablespoon Powdered
  Sugar
1 Dash Raspberry Syrup
Juice of ½ Lemon

Shake with ice and strain.
Fill with Soda Water.

ALEXANDER

1 jigger creme de cacao
1 jigger gin
1 jigger heavy cream

Shake w i t h cracked ice.
Strain.

ALEXANDER NO. 1

1 jigger Brandy
1 jigger Creme de Cacao
1 jigger Cream

Shake with ice and strain.

ALEXANDER NO. 2

1 jigger Dry Gin
½ jigger Creme de Cacao
½ jigger Cream

Shake with ice and strain.

ALFONSO SPECIAL

½ jigger Dry Gin
½ jigger Dry Vermouth
½ jigger Grand Marnier
4 Dashes Sweet Vermouth
1 Dash Angostura Bitters

Shake with ice and strain.

ALFONSO STANDARD
(CHAMPAGNE)

½ jigger Dubonnet
1 Cube Ice
1 Dash Bitters
1 Lump Sugar

Sprinkle with Bitters. Add
Ice and Dubonnet and fill
with iced Champagne. Serve
with twist of Lemon Peel.

ALASKA COCKTAIL

2 jiggers Gin
1 jigger Yellow Chartreuse
2 Dashes Orange
  Bitters

Stir with ice. Strain. Serve
with a twist of lemon peel.

ALICE MINE

1 jigger Dry Vermouth
4 Dashes Sweet Vermouth
2 jiggers Grand Marnier
1 jigger Dry Gin
1 Dash Angostura Bitters
Stir with ice and strain.

ALICE STANDARD

1 jigger Scotch
½ jigger Kummel
½ jigger Sweet Vermouth

Stir with ice. Strain.

ALLEN SPECIAL

1 jigger Dry Gin
½ jigger Maraschino
1 Dash Lemon Juice

Stir with ice and strain.

ALLIES

1 jigger Gin
1 jigger Dry Vermouth
2 Dashes Kummel

Sitr with ice and strain.

AMERICAN BEAUTY

1 jigger Brandy
1 jigger Dry Vermouth
1 jigger Orange Juice
1 Dash White Creme de
   Menthe
1 Dash Grenadine

Shake with ice and strain.
Top with a little Port.

AMERICAN FIZZ

1 jigger Gin
1 jigger Brandy
Juice of ½ Lemon
1 Teaspoon Grenadine

Shake with ice and strain.

AMERICAN ROSE

1 jigger Brandy
1 Dash Pernod
1 Teaspoon Grenadine
2 Slices of Ripe Peach,
   crushed with a fork

Shake with crushed ice and
strain. Fill w i t h chilled
Champagne.

AMERICANO

2 jigger Sweet Vermouth
1 jigger Campari

Add 2 ice cubes and a twist
of Lemon Peel. Fill with
Soda Water

ANGEL FACE

1 jigger Dry Gin
1 jigger Apricot Brandy
1 jigger Calvados or Apple
   Brandy

Stir with ice and strain.

3

ANGEL'S TIP

1 jigger Creme de Cacao
1/3 jigger Cream

Pour carefully into cordial glass in order given, so ingredients do not mix.

ANGOSTURA HIGHBALL

1 Teaspoon Angostura Bitters
2 cubes of ice, and fill up with Ginger Ale.

ANNIVERSARY COCKTAIL

½ jigger Gin
½ jigger Brandy
2 Dashes Orange Bitters

Shake with cracked ice and strain.

APPLE

1/3 jigger Gin
1 jigger Calvados or Applejack
1 jigger Apple Cider
½ jigger Brandy

Shake w i t h cracked ice. Strain into sour glass.

APPLE BLOW

2 jiggers Applejack
4 Dashes Lemon Juice
1 Teaspoon Sugar
1 Egg White

Shake with ice and strain. Fill with Soda Water.

APPLE BRANDY

1 jigger Apple Brandy
½ jigger Brandy
½ jigger Gin
1 jigger Sweet Cider

Stir with ice and strain.

APPLE CAR

1/3 jigger Triple Sec or Cointreau
1/3 jigger applejack
1/3 jigger lime juice

Shake with cracked ice and strain.

APPLEJACK NO. 1

1 jigger Applejack
1 Teaspoon Sugar Syrup
2 Dashes Orange Bitters
1 Dash Angostura Bitters

Shake with ice and strain Decorate w i t h fruit if desired.

APPLEJACK NO. 2

3 jiggers Apple Brandy
1 jigger Sweet Vermouth
1 Dash Angostura Bitters

Stir with ice and strain.

APPLEJACK COOLER

1 Tablespoon Sugar
Juice of ½ Lemon
1 or 2 jiggers Applejack

Shake with cracked ice and strain. Add ice cubes and fill with Soda Water.

APPLEJACK SOUR (DELMONICO)

2 jiggers Applejack
Juice of ½ Lime
Juice of ½ Lemon
1 Dash Grenadine
½ Teaspoon Sugar

APRICOT

1 jigger Apricot Brandy
½ jigger Orange Juice
½ jigger Lemon Juice
1 Dash Dry Gin

Shake with ice and strain.

APRICOT COOLER

1 jigger Apricot Brandy
Juice of ½ each Lemon and
  Lime
2 Dashes Grenadine

Shake with cracked ice and strain and fill w i t h Soda Water.

APPETIZER

1 jigger Whiskey
3 Dashes Curacao
2 Dashes Bitters
1 Twist Lemon Peel
1 Twist Orange Peel

Shake over ice. Strain.

APPETIZER NO. 1

1 jigger Dubonnet
Juice of ½ Orange

Shake with ice and strain.

AQUARIAN SPECIAL

1 jigger Gin
1 jigger Forbidden Fruit
1 jigger Cointreau

Shake with shaved ice and strain into Martini. Serve with olive.

5

ASSOCIATION SPECIAL

1 jigger Gin
½ jigger Sweet Vermouth
1 Dash Bitters

Stir with ice. Strain ice cubes and serve with a twist of lemon peel.

ATTA BOY

1 jigger Dry Gin
½ jigger Dry Vermouth
4 Dashes Grenadine

Stir with ice and strain. Serve with a twist of Lemon Peel.

ATTENTION

1 jigger Gin
1 jigger Ansone or Abisante
1 jigger Creme de Noya
2 Dashes Orange Bitters

Stir with ice and strain.

AROUND THE WORLD COCKTAIL

1 jigger Gin
1 jigger Green Creme de Menthe
1 jigger Pineapple Juice

Shake with cracked ice. Strain.

ARTIST'S SPECIAL

1 jigger Whiskey
1 jigger Sherry
½ jigger Sugar Syrup
½ jigger Lemon Juice

Stir with ice and strain.

ASTORIA

2 jiggers Dry Gin
1 jigger Dry Vermouth
1 Dash Orange Bitters

Stir with ice and strain. Serve with an Olive.

ATTY

2 jiggers Dry Gin
½ jigger Dry Vermouth
3 Dashes Creme de Violette

Stir well with ice and strain into glass. Serve with a twist of Lemon Peel.

AUNT JEMIMA

1 jigger Brandy
1 jigger Creme de Cacao
1 jigger Benedictine

Pour carefully so that they are in separate layers.

BACARDI STANDARD

2 jiggers Bacardi Rum
Juice of ½ Lime
2 Dashes Sugar Syrup

Shake with ice and strain.

BACARDI RUTH SPECIAL

2 jiggers Light Rum
1 jigger English Gin
Juice of ½ Lime
1 Teaspoon Grenadine

Shake with ice and strain.
Fill with Coke.

BACARDI FIZZ

2 jiggers Bacardi Rum
1 Teaspoon Sugar
Juice of ½ Lemon

Shake with ice and strain.
Fill with Soda Water.

BABBIE'S SPECIAL

2 jiggers Apricot Brandy
1 jigger Cream
1 Dash Gin

Shake with ice and strain.

BALD HEAD

1 jigger French Vermouth
1 jigger Italian Vermouth
4 jiggers Gin
1 or 2 Dashes Absinthe to
each drink

Stir with large cubes of ice.
Twist lemon peel over the
drink. Decorate w i t h a
stuffed olive.

BALTIMORE BRACER

1 jigger Brandy
1 jigger Anisette
1 Egg White

Shake with ice and strain.

BAMBOO

1 jigger Sherry
1 jigger Sweet Vermouth
1 Dash Bitters

Stir with ice and strain.

BARBARA

1 jigger Vodka
½ jigger Creme de Cacao
½ jigger Cream

Stir with ice and strain.

7

BARBARY COAST

1 jigger Gin
1 jigger Scotch
1 jigger Creme de Cacao
1 jigger Cream

Shake with ice and strain.

BARBOTAGE OF CHAMPAGNE

Fill tumbler ½ full of finely cracked ice. Add 1 dash of Angostura Bitters. 1 teaspoon each of Sugar Syrup and Lemon Juice fill with iced Champagne. Stir lightly and serve w i t h twist of Orange Peel.

BARNEY BARNATO

1 jigger Brandy
1 jigger Dubonnet
1 Dash Angostura Bitters
1 Dash Curacao

Stir with ice and strain.

BARNEY FRENCH

Place 1 slice Orange, 2 dashes Peychaud's Bitters, 1 twist Lemon Peel, 1 or 2 cubes Ice in an Old-Fashioned glass and muddle. Add 1 or 2 jiggers Whiskey and serve.

BARKING DOG

1 jigger Gin
1 jigger Dry Vermouth
1 jigger Sweet Vermouth
2 Dashes Bitters

Stir with ice and strain. Serve with cherry.

BARNUM

1½ jiggers Gin
1 jigger Apricot Brandy
2 Dashes Bitters
1 Dash Lemon or Lime juice

Shake with ice and strain.

BARTENDER'S SPECIAL

4 jiggers Gin
1 jigger Passion-Fruit Nectar
1 Dash Angostura
½ Lemon Juice

Stir with ice and strain. Serve with olive.

BARTON SPECIAL

1 jigger Apple Brandy
½ jigger Scotch Whisky
½ jigger Dry Gin

Shake with ice and strain. Serve with twist of Lemon Peel.

8

BASIC EGGNOG

2 jiggers Brandy or Light Rum, 1 Egg, 1 tablespoon Sugar and ¾ cup Milk. Shake and strain. Sprinkle with Nutmeg.

BEACHCOMBER

1½ jiggers Light Rum
½ jigger Cointreau
Juice of ½ Lime
2 Dashes Maraschino

Shake with shaved ice.

BEE'S KISS

1 jigger Rum
1 Teaspoon Honey
1 Teaspoon Cream

Shake with ice and strain.

BEES' KNEES

1 jigger Gin
1 Teaspoon Honey
Juice of ¼ Lemon

Shake with ice and strain.

BELMONT

2 jiggers Gin
1 jigger Grenadine or Raspberry Syrup
½ jigger Cream

Shake with ice and strain.

BERMUDA HIGHBALL

1 jigger Dry Gin
1 jigger Brandy
½ jigger Dry Vermouth

Combine in highball glass, with ice cubes, and fill with Ginger Ale or Soda Water. Garnish with Lemon Peel and serve.

BENEDICTINE

2 jiggers Benedictine
Dash Angostura Bitters

Rub rim with Lemon and dip in powder sugar. Shake and strain. Serve with Cherry

BENEDICTINE FRAPPE

Fill large cocktail glass with s h a v e d ice. Fill with Benedictine.

9

BENNETT

3 jiggers Dry Gin
1 jigger Lime Juice
1-2 Dashes Angostura
    Bitters
1 Teaspoon Powdered Sugar

Shake with ice and strain.

BENTLEY

1 jigger Calvados or Apple
    Brandy
1 jigger Dubonnet

Stir with ice and strain.

BERMUDA ROSE

1 jigger Dry Gin
1 Dash Grenadine
1 Dash Apricot Brandy
1/3 jigger Lemon or Lime
    juice

Shake with ice and strain.

BERRY WALL

1 jigger Dry Gin
1 jigger Sweet Vermouth
4 Dashes Curacao

Stir w i t h ice and strain.
Twist a Lemon Peel just over
the top and serve with a
Cherry.

BEST HOME-MADE

1-2 jiggers Gin
Juice of ½ Orange

Shake with ice and strain.

BETSY ROSS

1 jigger Brandy
1 jigger Port
2 Dashes Angostura Bitters
1 Dash Curacao

Stir with ice and strain.

BETWEEN-THE-SHEETS

1 jigger Brandy
1 jigger Cointreau
1 jigger Light Rum

Shake with ice and strain.

BETTER THAN ANYTHING

2 jiggers Brandy
1 Tablespoon Grenadine
1 Tablespoon Curacao
2 jiggers Cherry Brandy
1 Tablespoon Lemon Juice

Shake with cracked ice.

BICH'S SPECIAL

2 jiggers Dry Gin
1 jigger Lillet
1 Dash Angostura Bitters

Stir with ice and strain.
Squeeze Orange Peel over
top.

BIFFY

2 jiggers Dry Gin
1 jigger Swedish Punch
1 jigger Lemon Juice

Stir with ice and strain.

BIG BOY

2 jiggers Brandy
1 jigger Cointreau
1 jigger Sirop de Citron

Stir with ice and strain.

BIJOU

1 jigger Gin
1 jigger Green Chartreuse
1 jigger Sweet Vermouth
1 Dash Orange Bitters

Stir with ice. Strain. Serve
with a twist of lemon peel.

BISHOP

Fill tumbler ½ full with
cracked ice. 1 teaspoon
Sugar, Juice of ½ Lemon,
Juice of ½ Orange fill with
Burgundy or Claret. Stir and
add 1 slice of Orange and
several dashes of Rum.

BISMARCK FIZZ (SLOE GIN FIZZ)

2 jiggers Sloe Gin
Juice of ½ Lemon

Shake with ice and strain.
Fill with Soda Water.

BITTERSWEET

1 jigger Whiskey
Juice 1 Orange
½ Teaspoon Fine
   Granulated Sugar
2 Dashes Bitters

Shake with ice and strain.

BLACKTHORN

1 jigger Irish Whiskey
1 jigger Dry Vermouth
3 Dashes Pernod
3 Dashes Angostura Bitters

Stir with ice and strain.

11

BLACK COW

Fill a tall glass ¾ full of Sarsaparilla and add 1 or 2 scoops of Vanilla Ice Cream.

BLACK RUSSIAN

1 jigger coffee liqueur
1 jigger vodka

Pour over ice cubes in old-fashioned glass. Stir.

BLACK AND TAN

Fill tall glass, with 1 to 2 ice cubes, 2/3 full of Cola. Fill up with Milk. Stir and serve.

BLACK ROSE

1 jigger Rum
1 Teaspoon Sugar
Cold Black Coffee

Combine over ice. Stir and serve.

BLACK VELVET

Tall glass add half chilled Guinness' s t o u t and half chilled c h a m p a g n e. Stir quickly.

BLANCHE

1 jigger Cointreau
1 jigger Anisette
1 jigger White Curacao

Shake with ice and strain.

BLINKER

1 jigger Whiskey
1½ jigger Grapefruit Juice
½ jigger Grenadine

Shake with ice and strain.

BLOCK AND FALL

1 jigger Brandy
1 jigger Cointreau
½ jigger Apple Brandy
½ jigger Pernod

Shake with ice and strain.

BLOOD AND SAND

1 jigger Scotch
¾ jigger Cherry Brandy
¾ jigger Sweet Vermouth
¾ jigger Orange Juice

Stir well with ice. Strain into cocktail glass.

BLOODY MARIA

1 jigger Tequila
2 jiggers tomato juice
½ Ounce Lemon Juice
Dash salt
Dash Tabasco
Dash Worcestershire

Shake with cracked ice and strain.

BOBBY BURNS COCKTAIL

1 jigger Scotch
1 jigger Dry Vermouth
1 jigger Sweet Vermouth
1 Dash Claristine or
   Benedictine

Stir with ice. Strain.

BLUE DEVIL

1 jigger Gin
½ jigger Maraschino
½ jigger Lemon or Lime
   Juice
1 Dash Blue Vegetable
   Extract

Shake with ice and strain.

BOLERO

1 jigger Sugar Syrup
2 jiggers Lime Juice
4 jiggers Gold Label Cuban
   Rum
4 jiggers Cognac
1 Teaspoon Orange Juice to
   each drink

   Shake with finely crushed ice.

BLUE MOON

1 jigger Dry Gin
1/3 jigger Maraschino
1 Egg White

Shake with ice and strain.

BOLO

2 jiggers Light Rum
Juice of ½ Lemon or Lime
Juice of ¼ Orange
1 Teaspoon Powdered
   Sugar

Shake with ice and strain.

BLUE TRAIN

½ jigger Dry Gin
¼ jigger Lemon Juice
¼ jigger Cointreau
1 Dash Blue Vegetable
   Extract

Shake with ice and strain.

BOILERMAKER

Serve 1 l a r g e jigger of Whiskey straight, with a Beer chaser on the side.

13

BOMBAY

1 jigger Brandy
½ jigger Sweet Vermouth
½ jigger Dry Vermouth
2 Dashes Curacao
1 Dash Pernod

Stir with ice and strain.

BON APPETIT

1 jigger Dry Gin
1 jigger Dubonnet
3 Dashes Angostura Bitters
Juice of ½ Orange

Shake with ice and strain.

BONSONI

2 jiggers Sweet Vermouth
1 jigger Fernet Branca

Stir with ice and strain.

BOOMERANG

½ jigger Rye Whiskey
½ jigger Swedish Punch
½ jigger Dry Vermouth
1 Dash Lemon Juice

Stir with ice and strain.

BOOSTER

2 jiggers Brandy
4 Dashes Curacao
1 Egg White

Shake with ice and strain.
Serve with a grating of
Nutmeg.

BOURBON

1/3 jigger Benedictine
½ jigger Curacao
3 jiggers Bourbon
½ jigger Lemon Juice
1 Dash Angostura to each
   drink

Shake with cracked ice.

BOSOM CARESSER

2 jiggers Brandy
1 jigger Curacao
1 Teaspoon Grenadine
1 Egg Yolk

Shake with ice and strain.

BRAINSTORM

1 jigger Whiskey
2 Dashes Dry Vermouth
2 Dashes Claristine or
   Benedictine
1 Twist Orange Peel

Pour ingredients in Old Fashioned glass over ice cubes and stir.

14

BRANDY BLAZER

Combine in a small thick glass 2 jiggers Brandy, 1 lump Sugar and 1 twist of Orange Pee!. Blaze the Brandy and strain.

BRANDY COBBLER

Fill a tumbler ¾ full of cracked ice. Add 1 teaspoon Curacao, ½ Teaspoon Sugar, 2 jiggers Brandy. Decorate with fruit.

BRANDY

2/3 jigger Brandy
½ Teaspoon Sugar or Simple Syrup
1 Dash Bitters

Stir with cubes of ice. Strain and add twist of lemon.

BRANDY DAISY

1 jigger of Brandy
Juice of ½ Lemon
4 Dashes Grenadine

Pour into a glass filled with fine ice and fill with soda. Garnish with fresh fruit.

BRANDY FLIP

1½ jiggers Brandy
1 Teaspoon Sugar or Simple Syrup
1 Whole Egg

Shake with cracked ice and strain into cocktail glass. Decorate with grated nutmeg.

BRANDY FIZZ

2 jiggers Brandy
1 Tablespoon Powdered Sugar
Juice of ½ Lemon
Juice of ½ Lime

Shake with ice and strain. Fill up with Soda Water.

BRANDY FIX

1 jigger Brandy
1 jigger Cherry Brandy
1 Teaspoon Sugar
1 Teaspoon Water
Juice of ½ Lemon

Moisten the Sugar with the Water and add the other ingredients. Fill with ice and and stir. Add a slice of Lemon or twist of Peel. Serve with a straw.

BRANDY OLD-FASHIONED

Place lump of Sugar in bottom of Old-Fashioned glass. Sprinkle with 1 d a s h of Angostura Bitters. Add twist of Lemon Peel and ice cubes and f i l l as desired with Brandy. Stir and serve.

BRANDY SLING

Place in a highball glass 3 cubes of Ice, 1 dash Angostura Bitters, the juice of ½ Lemon, 1 t e a s p o o n Sugar and 2 jiggers Brandy. Fill with plain Water, stir and serve.

BRANDY SPECIAL

2 jiggers Brandy
2 Dashes Curacao
2 Dashes Sugar Syrup
2 Dashes Bitters
1 Twist of Lemon Peel

Stir with ice and strain.

BRANDY VERMOUTH

3 jiggers Brandy
1 jigger Sweet Vermouth
1 Dash Angostura Bitters

Stir with ice and strain

BRAVE BULL

1 jigger Tequila
1 jigger Coffee Liqueur

Pour over ice cubes in old-fashioned glass. Add twist of lemon.

BRAZIL

1 jigger Sherry
1 jigger Dry Vermouth
1 Dash Pernod
1 Dash Angostura Bitters

Stir well with ice and strain into glass. Squeeze Lemon Peel over top.

BREAKFAST

1 jigger Dry Gin
1 jigger Grenadine
1 Egg White

Shake with ice and strain.

BREAKFAST EGGNOG

1 Fresh Egg
¾ jigger Brandy
¼ jigger Curacao
¼ Glass Milk

Shake with ice and strain. Grate Nutmeg on top.

16

BROKEN SPUR

2 jiggers White Port
½ Dry Gin
½ jigger Sweet Vermouth
1 Egg Yolk
1 Teaspoon Anisette

Shake with ice and strain.

BROADWAY SMILE

1 jigger Cointreau
1 jigger Swedish Punch
1 jigger Creme de Casses

Pour carefully into liqueur glass so that ingredients do not mix.

BRONX

1½ jigger gin
½ jigger French vermouth
½ jigger Italian vermouth
½ jigger Orange Juice

Shake w i t h cracked ice. Strain i n t o cocktail glass. Drop twist of orange peel into glass.

BRONX (DRY)

2 jiggers Gin
½ jigger Dry Vermouth
Juice of ¼ Orange

Stir with ice and strain.

BRONX (SWEET)

1½ jigger Gin
½ jigger Dry Vermouth
½ jigger Sweet Vermouth
Juice of ¼ Orange

Stir with ice and strain.

BRONX RIVER

3 jiggers Dry Gin
1 jigger Sweet Vermouth
Juice of 1 Lemon
½ Teaspoon Sugar

Stir with ice and strain.

BROOKLYN

1½ jigger Whiskey
½ jigger Dry Vermouth
1 Dash Maraschino
1 Dash Bitters

Stir with ice and strain.

BROOKLYN (GIN)

1½ jigger Gin
½ jigger Sweet Vermouth
2 Dashes Orange Juice
½ Egg White
Nutmeg

Shake with ice. Strain into cocktail glass. Add grated nutmeg.

17

BULLDOG

1½ jigger Gin
Juice of 1 Orange

Stir with ice in large Old Fashioned glass. Fill with ginger ale.

BUBY

1 jigger Dry Gin
1 jigger Lemon Juice
1 Teaspoon Grenadine

Shake and strain.

BUNNY HUG

1 jigger Gin
1 jigger Whiskey
1 jigger Abisante or
    Anesone

Shake with ice and strain.

BUCKS FIZZ

1 jigger Gin
½ Teaspoon Sugar
Juice of ½ Orange

Shake with ice and strain. Fill with chilled Champagne.

BUTTON HOOK

1 jigger Pernod
1 jigger Apricot Brandy
1 jigger Brandy
1 jigger White Creme de
    Menthe

Shake with ice and strain.

B.V.D.

½ jigger Gin
½ jigger light Rum
½ jigger Dry Vermouth

Stir with ice and strain.

BYCULLA

1 jigger Sherry
1 jigger Port
1 jigger Curacao
1 jigger Ginger

Stir with ice and strain.

BYRRH

1 jigger Byrrh
1 jigger Rye Whiskey
1 Dry Vermouth

Stir with ice and strain.

BYRRH CASSES

1 jiggers Byrrh
1 jigger Creme de Cassis

Fill with Soda Water.

18

BYRRH COCKTAIL

½ jigger Byrrh
½ jigger Dry Vermouth
½ jigger Scotch

Stir with ice and strain.

BYRRH SPECIAL

1 jigger Byrrh
1 jigger Old Tom Gin

Stir with ice and strain.

CABARET

1 jigger Dry Gin
1 jigger Dubonnet
1 Dash Pernod
1 Dash Angostura Bitters

Stir with ice and strain. Serve
with a Cherry.

CABLEGRAM

1 jigger Whiskey
1 Teaspoon Powdered Sugar
Juice of ½ Lemon

Stir with ice. Strain into 4
oz. cocktail glass. Fill with
ginger ale.

CAFE KIRSCH

1 jigger Kirsch
1 Teaspoon Sugar
2 jiggers Cold Coffee
1 Egg White

Shake with ice and strain.

CAFE DE PARIS

2 jiggers Dry Gin
3 Dashes Anisette
1 Teaspoon Cream
1 Egg White

Shake with ice and strain.

CAFE ROYALE

An individual cup of hot
coffee flamed with a spirit
kirsch, cognac, bourbon, or
151 p r o o f Ronrico rum.
Place a cube of sugar in a
teaspoon. Fill spoon with
liquor, d o u s i n g the sugar.
Hold teaspoon over cup of
hot c o f f e e and set spirit
aflame. Dip spoon in coffee
and stir.

CALIFORNIA LEMONADE

1 jigger Rye Whiskey
1 Dash Grenadine
Juice of 1 Lemon
Juice of 1 Lime
1 T a b l e s p o o n Powdered
  Sugar

Shake with ice and strain.
Fill w i t h chilled Soda
Water.

CALISAY

1 jigger Calisay
1 jigger Sweet Vermouth
3 Dashes Sugar Syrup

Stir with ice and strain.

CALVADOS

1 jigger Calvados or Apple
  Brandy
1 jigger Orange Juice
½ jigger Cointreau
½ jigger Orange Bitters

Stir with ice and strain.

CAPETOWN

½ jigger Whiskey
½ jigger Dry Vermouth
3 Dashes Curacao
1 Dash Bitters

Stir with ice. Strain into
cocktail glass. Serve with
twist of lemon peel.

CASINO

2 jiggers Gin
2 Dashes Maraschino
2 Dashes Orange Bitters
2 Dashes Lemon Juice

Stir with ice and strain.

CANADIAN NO. 1

1 jigger Curacao
3 Dashes Jamaica Rum
1 Teaspoon Powdered
  Sugar
Juice of ½ Lemon

Shake with ice and strain.

CANADIAN NO. 2

1 jigger Canadian Club Whiskey
1 Dash Curacao
2 Dashes Angostura Bitters
1 Teaspoon Powdered Sugar

Shake with ice and strain.

CASTLE DIP

1 jigger Apple Brandy
1 jigger White Creme de
  Menthe
3 Dashes Pernod

Shake with ice and strain.

CHAMPAGNE COBBLER

Fill large goblet 2/3 full of cracked ice. Add ½ teaspoon Lemon Juice and ½ teaspoon Curacao. Stir and add 1 thin slice of Orange and 1 small Pineapple stick. Fill with iced Champagne. Stir again and serve.

CHAMPAGNE COCKTAIL

Champagne
1 Lump Sugar
1 Dash Bitters
1 Twist Lemon Peel
1 Twist Orange Peel

CHAMPAGNE COOLER

Place in tall glass, ½ filled with ice, 2/3 jigger Brandy 2/3 jigger Cointreau and fill with chilled Champagne. Stir and garnish with Mint.

CHAMPAGNE FIZZ

Juice of 1 Orange. Highball glass with several ice cubes. Fill with iced Champagne.

CHAMPAGNE JULEP

Crush 4 sprigs Mint with 1 lump of Sugar and a few drops of water in bottom of tall highball glass. Half fill with cracked ice and add 1 jigger Brandy. Fill with Champagne and decorate with extra Mint.

CHAMPAGNE VELVET (BLACK VELVET)

Half fill a tall glass with iced Stout. Fill with iced Champagne. Pour slowly.

CARROL COCKTAIL

2 jiggers Brandy
1 jigger Sweet Vermouth

Stir with ice and strain. Serve with onion.

CHARLESTON

½ jigger Dry Gin
½ jigger Kirsch
½ jigger Maraschino
½ jigger Curacao
½ jigger Dry Vermouth
½ jigger Sweet Vermouth

Stir with ice and strain into glass. Squeeze Lemon Peel over top.

CHARLIE LINDBERGH

1 jigger English Gin
1 jigger Lillet
2 Dashes Apricot Brandy
2 Dashes Orange Juice

Stir with ice and strain into glass. Squeeze Lemon Peel over top.

CHANTICLEER

2 jiggers Dry Gin
Juice of ½ Lemon
1 Tablespoon Raspberry
    Syrup
1 Egg White

Shake with ice and strain.

CHICAGO COCKTAIL

1 jigger Brandy
1 Dash Curacao
1 Dash Bitters
Champagne

Stir with ice. Strain into Champagne g l a s s frosted sugar rim. Fill with iced Champagne.

CHRYSANTHEMUM

1 jigger Dry Vermouth
1 jigger Benedictine
3 Dashes Pernod

Stir with ice and strain. Serve with twist of Orange Peel.

CITY SLICKER

2 jiggers Brandy
1 jigger Curacao
1 Dash Pernod

Shake with ice and strain.

CINCINNATI

Fill a highball glass ½ full of Beer. Fill with chilled Soda Water.

CLARET COBBLER

Fill tumbler ½ full of cracked ice. Add 1 dash Maraschino, 1 teaspoon each Sugar and Lemon Juice. Fill with Claret and stir. Decorate with fruit.

CLARIDGE

½ jigger Gin
½ jigger Dry Vermouth
½ jigger Apricot Brandy

Stir with ice. Strain. Serve with cherry.

CLARIDGE

1 jigger Dry Gin
1 jigger Dry Vermouth
½ jigger Apricot Brandy
½ jigger Cointreau

Stir with ice and strain. Serve with a cherry.

CLASSIC

2 jiggers Brandy
½ jigger Curacao
½ jigger Maraschino
½ jigger Lemon Juice

Stir with ice and strain.

CLOAK AND DAGGER

Fill a highball glass with ice cubes. Add 1-½ jiggers Jamaica Rum and fill with Cola. Add twist of Orange Peel and a dash of Orange Bitters.

CLOUD 9

1 jigger Pernod
1 Dash Peychaud Bitters
1 Dash Orange Bitters
¼ Teaspoon Sugar or Simple Syrup

Place bitters and sugar in tall glass, fill with cracked ice. Pour in Pernod and one ounce of water. Stir gently.

CLOVER CLUB

1 jigger Gin
4 Dashes Grenadine
Juice of ½ Lemon
1 Egg White

Shake with ice and strain.

COLUMBIA COCKTAIL

1 jigger Rum
½ jigger Raspberry Syrup
1/3 jigger Lemon Juice

Shake with ice and strain.

COFFEE NO. 1

1 jigger Brandy
1 jigger Cointreau
1 jigger Cold Black Coffee

Shake with ice and strain.

COFFEE NO. 2

2 jiggers Brandy
1 jigger Port
2 Dashes Curacao
2 Dashes Sugar Syrup
1 Egg Yolk

Shake with ice and strain. Serve with a grating of Nutmeg.

COLONIAL

1 jigger Gin
½ jigger Grapefruit Juice
3 Dashes Maraschino

Shake with ice and strain.

23

COMMODORE

1½ jigger Whiskey
Juice of ½ Lime or
   Juice of ¼ Lemon
2 Dashes Orange Bitters
1 Teaspoon Sugar Syrup

Shake with ice and strain.

CONTINENTAL

½ jigger Sweet Cream
1 jigger Lemon Juice
3 Jiggers Rye
3 Dashes Jamaica Rum to
   each drink
Shake with crushed ice.

COOPERSTOWN

1 jigger Dry Gin
½ jigger Dry Vermouth
½ jigger Sweet Vermouth
1 Sprig Fresh Mint

Stir well with ice and strain
into glass. Serve with a small
sprig of Mint or a Cherry.

CORDOVA

2 jiggers Dry Gin
1 jigger Sweet Vermouth
1 Dash Pernod
1 Teaspoon Cream

Shake with ice and strain.

CORNELL

1 jigger Dry Gin
3 Dashes Maraschino
1 Egg White

Shake with ice and strain.

CORONATION NO. 1

1 jigger Sherry
1 jigger Dry Vermouth
1 Dash Maraschino
2 Dashes Orange Bitters

CORONATION NO. 2

2 jiggers Brandy
1 jigger Curacao
1 Dash Peach Bitters
1 Dash White Creme de Menthe

Stir with ice and strain.

CORPSE REVIVER

1 jigger Dry Gin
1 jigger Cointreau
1 jigger Swedish Punch
1 jigger Lemon Juice
1 Dash Pernod

Shake with ice and strain.

COSSACK

½ jigger Sugar Syrup
1 jigger Lime Juice
2 jiggers Vodka
2 jiggers Cognac

Shake with crushed ice.

COUNTRY COOLER

2 jiggers Dry Vermouth
1 Teaspoon Grenadine

Place in tall glass with ice and fill with Soda Water.

COWBOY

2 jiggers Whiskey
1 jigger Cream

Shake with shaved ice and strain

CREOLE COCKTAIL

½ jigger Extra
½ jigger Sweet Vermouth
2 Dashes Claristine or Benedictin
2 Dashes Bitters

Stir with ice. Strain. Serve with twist of lemon peel.

CROWN COCKTAIL

1 jigger Whiskey
½ jigger Lemon Juice
1 Dash Grenadine

Stir with ice and strain.

CROW

2 jiggers Whiskey
1 jigger Lemon Juice
1 Dash Grenadine

Stir with ice and strain.

CUBA LIBRE (RUM AND COCA-COLA)

1½ jiggers Puerto Rican White Lable Rum
Juice of one small lime
Cola drink

Tall glass. 3 ice cubes and fill with cola. Stir.

CUBAN COOLER

Place ice cubes in tall highball glass. Add 1½ jiggers Rum and fill with Ginger Ale. Garnish with twist of Lemon Peel.

CUBANO

1 jigger Dry Gin
1 jigger Dry Vermouth
4 Drops Kummel
4 Drops Charbreux
2 Drops Pineapple Syrup

Shake with ice and strain.

CULROSS

1 jigger Apricot Brandy
1 jigger Light Rum
1 jigger Lillet
Juice of ¼ Lemon

Stir with ice and strain.

CUPID

2 jiggers Sherry
1 Egg
1 Teaspoon Powdered Sugar
1 Pinch Cayenne Pepper

Shake with ice and strain.

CZARINA

½ jigger French Vermouth
½ jigger Italian Vermouth
3 jiggers Vodka
1 jigger Apricot Brandy

DAIQUIRI BANANA

1½ jigger Rum
Juice of ½ Lime
½ oz. Banana Liqueur
   (or one teaspoon sugar)
½ ripe banana

Blend with cracked ice.

DAIQUIRI (FROZEN)

1 jigger Light Rum
1 Tablespoon Lime or
   Lemon Juice
2 Teaspoons Powdered
   Sugar
Blend 2 cups shaved ice with
ingredients until consistency
of snow. Serve with straw.

DAIQUIRI STANDARD

1½ jigger Rum
Juice of ½ Lime
1 Teaspoon Sugar

Shake with ice. Pour into
cocktail glass.

DAIQUIRI DE LUXE

1 jigger Orgeat or Creme
   d' Ananas
1½ jigger Citrus Juice of
   Large Lemon and three
   Large Limes
3 jiggers Cuban White Label
   Bacardi or Havana Club
   Rum

DAIQUIRI NACIONAL

1 jigger White Label Rum
1 jigger Arpicot Brandy
½ Lime
1 Teaspoon Sugar

Blend with cracked ice.

DAIQUIRI PEACH

1 jigger Rum
Juice of ½ Lime
1/3 jigger Peach Liqueur
2 Canned peach halves

Blend with cracked ice.

DANDY

½ jigger Extra
½ jigger Dry Vermouth
1 Dash Bitters
3 Dashes Triple Sec
1 Twist each Lemon
   and Orange Peel

Stir with ice and strain.

DARB

1 jigger Dry Gin
1 jigger Dry Vermouth
1 jigger Apricot Brandy
4 Dashes Lemon Juice

Stir with ice and strain.

DARBY

1 jigger Gin
½ jigger Lime Juice
½ jigger Grapefruit Juice
1 Teaspoon Powdered Sugar

Shake with ice. Strain into
cocktail glass. Add cherry &
dash of Soda.

DAVIS

1 jigger Jamaica Rum
1 jigger Dry Vermouth
2 Dashes Raspberry Syrup
Juice of 1 Lime

Shake with ice and strain.

DAVIS BRANDY

2 jiggers Brandy
1 jigger Dry Vermouth
4 Dashes Grenadine
1 Dash Angostura Bitters

Stir with ice and strain.

DEMPSEY

1 jigger Dry Gin
1 jigger Calvados or Apple
   Brandy
2 Dashes Pernod
2 Dashes Grenadine

Stir with ice and strain.

DEPTH BOMB

1 jigger Applejack
1 jigger Brandy
¼ Teaspoon Grenadine
¼ Teaspoon Lemon Juice

Shake with ice and strain.

DEPTH CHARGE

1 jigger Dry Gin
1 jigger Lillet
2 Dashes Pernod

Shake with ice and strain.
Squeeze O r a n g e Peel over
top.

DERBY

1 jigger Extra
½ jigger Sweet Vermouth
½ jigger Curacao
Juice of ½ Lime

Shake with ice. Strain into
cocktail glass. Add mint leaf.

DERBY FIZZ

1 jigger Whiskey
5 Dashes Lemon Juice
1 Teaspoon Sugar
1 Egg
3 Dashes Curacao

Shake with ice and strain.
Fill with Soda Water.

DERBY NO. 2

1 jigger Whiskey
½ jigger Sweet Vermouth
½ jigger White Curacao
Juice of ½ Lime

Shake with ice and strain.
Add Mint Leaf.

DE RIGUEUR

1 jigger Whiskey
½ jigger Grapefruit Juice
1 Teaspoon Honey

Shake with ice and strain.

DESHLER

1 jigger Rye Whiskey
1 jigger Dubonnet
2 Dashes Peychaud's Bitters
2 Dashes Cointreau
2 Twists Orange Peel
1 Twist Lemon Peel

Shake with ice and strain.
Serve with a twist of Orange
Peel.

DEVIL'S

1 jigger Port
1 jigger Dry Vermouth
2 Dashes Lemon juice

Stir with ice and strain.

DIANA

3 jiggers White Creme de
   Menthe
1 jigger Brandy

Stir well with shaved ice and
strain.

DIABOLA

1 jigger Dry Gin
2 jiggers Dubonnet
2 Dashes Orgeat Syrup

Stir with ice and strain. Add
Cherry.

DICK MOLNAR

2 jiggers Calvados or Apple
   Brandy
½ jigger Swedish Punch
½ jigger Grapefruit Juice

Stir with ice and strain.

DIPLOMAT

2 jiggers Dry Vermouth
1 jigger Sweet Vermouth
1 Dash Maraschino

Stir with ice and strain. Add
Cherry and squeeze Lemon
Peel over top.

DIXIE

1 jigger Gin
½ jigger Anesone or Abisante
½ jigger Dry Vermouth
Juice of ¼ Orange
2 Dashes Grenadine

Shake with ice and strain.

DODGE SPECIAL

1 jigger Dry Gin
1 jigger Cointreau
1 Dash Grape Juice

Stir with ice and strain.

DOLLY O'DARE

1 jigger Dry Gin
1 jigger Dry Vermouth
6 Dashes Apricot Brandy

Stir w i t h ice and strain.
Squeeze O r a n g e Peel over
top.

DOUBLE TROUBLE

2 jiggers Brandy
1 jigger Dry Vermouth
4 Dashes Grenadine
1 Dash Angostura Bitters

Shake with ice and strain.

29

DOUGLAS

2 jiggers English Gin
1 jigger Dry Vermouth

Stir with ice and strain.
Squeeze Orange or Lemon
Peel over top.

DOWN THE HATCH

1 jigger Whiskey
3 Dashes Blackberry Brandy
2 Dashes Orange Bitters

Shake with ice and strain.

DREAM

2 jiggers Brandy
1 jigger Curacao
1 Dash Pernod

Stir with ice and strain.

DUBARRY

1 jigger Gin
½ jigger Dry Vermouth
2 Dashes Pernod
1 Dash Bitters

Stir with ice and strain. Add
thin slice of orange.

DUBONNET COCKTAIL

1 jigger Dubonnet
½ jigger Gin

Stir ice and strain. Twist of
lemon peel.

DUCHESS

1 jigger Pernod
1 jigger Dry Vermouth
1 jigger Sweet Vermouth

Shake with ice and strain.

DUKE OF MARLBOROUGH

1 jigger Sweet Vermouth
3 Dashes Raspberry Syrup
Juice of 1 Lime

Shake with ice and strain.

DUNLOP

2 jiggers Light Rum
1 jigger Sherry
1 Dash Angostura Bitters

Stir with ice and strain.

EARTHQUAKE COCKTAIL

1 jigger Whiskey
1 jigger Gin
1 jigger Anesone or Abisante

Shake with ice and strain.

EAST INDIAN

1 jigger Sherry
1 jigger Dry Vermouth
1 Dash Orange Bitters

Stir with ice and strain.

EL DIABOLO

1 jigger Tequila
1/3 jigger Creme de Cassis
½ Lime
Ginger Ale

Fill with Ginger Ale and stir.

EL PRESIDENTE EDWARDO

1½ jigger Gold Label Rum
½ jigger Curacao
½ jigger Dry Vermouth
1 Dash Grenadine

Shake with ice and strain.

EGG NOG STANDARD

1 Egg
1 Teaspoonful Sugar
1 jigger Liquor
4 jiggers Milk

Shake vigorously with cracked ice, strain into a tall glass, add a dash of nutmeg over the top.

ELK

½ jigger Dry Gin
½ jigger Prunelle Brandy
2 Dashes Dry Vermouth

Shake with ice and strain.

ELK COCKTAIL

1 jigger Extra
1 jigger Port
1 Egg White
Juice of ½ Lemon
1 Teaspoon Sugar

Shake with ice and strain. Add small wedge of pineapple.

EMPIRE

1 jigger Dry Gin
½ jigger Calvados or Apple Brandy
½ jigger Apricot Brandy

Stir with ice and strain. Serve with Cherry.

E. NOS

2 jiggers Dry Gin
1 jigger Dry Vermouth
3 Dashes Pernod

Stir with ice and strain. Serve with Cherry.

EVANS

2 jiggers Rye Whiskey
1 Dash Apricot Brandy
1 Dash Curacao

Stir with ice and strain.

ETON BLAZER COCKTAIL

3 jiggers English Gin
1 jigger Kirsch
½ Tablespoon Powdered
   Sugar
Juice of ½ Lemon

Shake and strain. Fill with
Soda.

EVERYTHING BUT

1 jigger Whiskey
1 jigger Gin
1 jigger Lemon Juice
1 jigger Orange Juice
1 Egg
1 Teaspoon Apricot Brandy
½ Teaspoon Powdered Sugar

Shake with ice. Strain into
sour glass.

EYEOPENER

1 jigger Light Rum
2 Dashes Creme De Noyau
2 Dashes Curacao
2 Dashes Pernod
1 Teaspoon Powdered Sugar
1 Egg Yolk

Shake with ice and strain.

FALLEN ANGEL

1 jigger Gin
Juice of 1 Lemon
or Lime
2 Dashes Creme de Menthe
1 Dash Bitters

Stir with ice. Strain. Serve
with cherry.

FANS

2 jiggers Scotch Whiskey
1 jigger Cointreau
1 jigger Unsweetened
   Grapefruit Juice

Shake with ice and strain.

FAIR AND WARMER

2 jiggers Light Rum
1 jigger Sweet Vermouth
2 Dashes Curacao

Stir with ice and strain. Serve
with twist of Lemon Peel.

FAIRBANKS NO. 1

1 jigger Dry Gin
1 jigger Dry Vermouth
1 jigger Apricot Brandy
1 Dash Lemon Juice
1 Dash Grenadine

Stir with ice and strain. Serve with Cherry.

FAIRBANKS NO. 2

2 jiggers Dry Gin
1 jigger Dry Vermouth
2 Dashes Orange Bitters
2 Dashes Creme de Noyau

Stir with ice and strain. Serve with Cherry.

FARE-THE-WELL

1 jigger Gin
1 jigger Dry Vermouth
2 Dashes Sweet Vermouth
6 Dashes Curacao

Shake with ice and strain.

FESTIVAL

½ jigger Apricot Brandy
½ jigger Creme de Cacao
½ jigger Cream
1 Teaspoon Grenadine

Shake with ice and strain.

FIESTA COCKTAIL

1 jigger Tequila
2 jiggers St. Raphael
½ jigger lime juice

Shake with cracked ice and strain. Garnish with maraschino cherry.

FIFTY-FIFTY

1 jigger Dry Gin
1 jigger Dry Vermouth

Stir with cracked ice and strain. Serve with Olive.

FINE AND DANDY

1 jigger English Gin
½ jigger Cointreau
½ jigger Lemon Juice
1 Dash Angostura Bitters

Stir with ice and strain. Serve with Cherry.

FIREMAN'S SOUR

1 jigger Rum
½ Teaspoon Powdered
   Sugar
Juice of 1 Lime
½ Oz. Grenadine

Shake with ice and strain. Decorate with orange and lime slices.

33

FLAMINGO

1 jigger Apricot Brandy
1 jigger Lime Juice
3 jiggers Gin
1 or 2 Dashes Grenadine to
   each drink

Shake with cracked ice.

FLYING SAUCER

1 jigger Rum
½ jigger Dry Vermouth
½ jigger Swedish Punch
1 Dash Grenadine

Shake w i t h cracked ice.
Strain into cocktail glass.

FLORIDA SPECIAL

1¼ jiggers Leilani Rum
1 Teaspoon Dry Vermouth
1 Teaspoon Sweet Vermouth
1 jigger Unsweetened
   Grapefruit Juice

Stir with shaved ice.   Strain
into cocktail glass.

FLYING SCOTCHMAN

1 jigger Scotch
½ jigger Italian Vermouth
1 Dash Bitters
1 Dash Sugar Syrup

shake with cracked ice.

FOG CUTTER

1 ½ jiggers Puerto Rican
   Rum
2/3 jigger Brandy
1/3 jigger Gin
2/3 jigger Orange Juice
1 Jigger Lemon Juice
1/3 jigger Orgeat Syrup
Sherry

FLU

1 jigger Whiskey
1 Teaspoon Ginger Brandy
1 Teaspoon Rock Candy
   Syrup
1 Teaspoon Light Rum
Juice of ¼ Lemon

Stir without ice. Strain.

Shake ingredients, e x c e p t
the Sherry, with cracked ice
and pour into a 14-ounce
glass.   Float the Sherry on
top.

FOURTH DEGREE

1 jigger Dry Gin
1 jigger Dry Vermouth
1 jigger Sweet Vermouth
4 Dashes Pernod

Stir with ice and strain. Serve with Cherry or a twist of Lemon Peel.

FOX RIVER

2 jiggers Whiskey
1 jigger Creme de Cacao
4 Dashes Peach Bitters

Stir gently with little ice. Strain i n t o cocktail glass. Squeeze lemon peel over top.

FOX TROT

1 jigger Rum
2 Dashes Curacao
Juice of ½ Lime or
    Lemon

Shake with ice and strain.

FRANKENJACK

1 jigger Dry Gin
1 jigger Dry Vermouth
½ jigger Apricot Brandy
½ jigger Cointreau

Stir with ice and strain. Serve with Cherry.

FRAPPE (PERNOD)

1 jigger Pernod
1/3 jigger Anisette
2 Dashes Angostura Bitters

Shake with shaved ice and strain.

FRED'S SPECIAL

2 jiggers Canadian Club
½ jigger Lemon Juice
1 Slice of Lemon

Stir with crushed ice. Pour and fill with coke.

FRENCH "75"

1 jigger Gin
½ jigger Lemon Juice
1 Teaspoon Powdered Sugar
Champagne

Pour over cracked ice. Stir. Fill with Champagne.

FRENCH ROSE

2 jiggers Dry Gin
1 jigger Cherry Brandy
1 jigger Cherry Liqueur

Shake with ice and strain.

FROTH BLOWER

1 jigger English Gin
1 Teaspoon Grenadine
1 Egg White

Shake with ice and strain.

FRISCO

1 jigger Benedictin
½ jigger Lemon Juice
3 jiggers Whiskey

Shake with cracked ice.

GASPER

1 jigger Dry Gin
1 jigger Apricot Brandy

Shake with ice and strain.

GEMINI ABA BOOSTER

1½ jiggers Gin
1½ jiggers Vodka
1 Dash Angostura Bitters
½ jigger Creme de Menthe

Shake with shaved ice and strain.

GENTLEMAN'S TODDY

½ jigger Jamaican Rum
½ jigger Puerto Rican Gold
  Label rum
½ Teaspoon Sugar
Thin slice of Lemon
1" Stick of Cinnamon
2 Whole Allspice

Use heavy glass cup or mug. Add 3 ounces boiling water. Stir. Twist lemon peel over cup but do not add.

GIBSON

1½ jiggers Gin
½ jigger Dry Vermouth

Stir with ice. Strain. Serve with pearl onion.

GIMLEY

1 jigger Gin or Vodka
1 Tablespoon Lime Juice
½ Teaspoon Sugar or
    Simple Syrup

Slice of Lime

Shake with ice and strain. Garnish with lime.

GIN FIZZ

2 jiggers Dry Gin
1 Tablespoon Powdered
    Sugar
Juice of ½ Lemon
Juice of ½ Lime

Shake with ice and strain into glass. Fill with Soda Water.

GIN 'N' SODA

1 jigger Gin
Soda

GIN 'N' BITTERS

Fill old-fashioned glass with gin to ¼" of top. Add bitters to taste. Stir. Twist of lemon and drop peel into glass.

Pour into highball glass full of ice. Fill with soda.

GIN 'N' TONIC

1 jigger Gin
¼ Lime
Tonic

GIN DAISY

1 jigger Gin
4 Dashes Grenadine
1/2 jigger Lemon Juice

Add finely cracked ice into mixing glass and shake well. Pour unstrained into highball glass. Decorate with fruit.

GIN PUNCH STANDARD

Place in a tall glass 1 lump Sugar, 1 twist Lemon Peel, Juice of ½ Lemon, 2 dashes Maraschino and 2 jiggers Dry Gin. Add cracked ice and fill with Soda Water. Stir and serve.

GIN ON THE ROCKS

1 jigger Gin

Pour over ice cubes in Old Fashioned glass. Add twist of lemon peel.

GIN RICKEY

1 jigger Gin
Juice of ½ Lime

Over ice cubes-fill with soda.

GIN RAPHAEL

1 jigger St. Raphael
½ jigger gin

Stir with ice and strain. Garnish with twist of orange peel.

GIN SOUR

1 jigger Gin
½ Teaspoon Sugar
Juice of ½ Lemon

Shake with ice. Serve in sour g l a s s. Garnish with cherry and orange slice.

GIN STINGER

2 jiggers Dry Gin
1 jigger White Creme de Menthe

Shake with shaved ice and strain.

GIN SWIZZLE

1 jigger Gin
¼ jigger Fresh Lime Juice
1 Teaspoon Fine Granulated Sugar
6 Dashes Bitters

Pour ingredients into pitcher. Add shaved ice. Mix vigorously until the pitcher begins to frost. Then strain into cocktail class and serve. Or serve with cracked ice in tall glass.

GLAD EYE

2 jiggers Pernod
1 jigger Peppermint

Shake with ice and strain.

GLOOM CHASER

1 jigger Grand Marnier
1 jigger Curacao
1 jigger Lemon Juice
1 jigger Grenadine

Stir with ice and strain.

GOLDEN CLIPPER

1 jigger Dry Gin
1 jigger Light Rum
1 jigger Peach Brandy
1 jigger Orange Juice

Shake with ice and strain.

GOLDEN DAWN

2/3 jigger Dry Gin
½ jigger Orange Juice
1/3 jigger Apricot Brandy

Shake with ice and strian.

GOLDEN ERMINE

2 jigger Dry Gin
1½ jigger Dry Vermouth
½ jigger Sweet Vermouth

Stir with ice and strain.

GOLDEN SLIPPER

½ jigger Yellow Chartreuse
½ jigger Eau de Vie Danzig
1 Egg Yolk

Shake with ice and strain.

GOLF

2 jiggers Dry Gin
1 jigger Dry Vermouth
2 Dashes Angostura Bitters

Stir with ice and strain. Serve with Olive.

GRAND SLAM

1 jigger Swedish Punch
½ jigger Sweet Vermouth
½ jigger Dry Vermouth

Stir with ice and strain.

GRADEAL SPECIAL

1 jigger Light Rum
½ jigger Apricot Brandy
½ jigger Dry Gin

Stir with ice and strain.

GRAND PASSION

1 jigger Passion-Fruit Nectar
3 jiggers Gin
1 Dash Angostura to each drink
½ Lemon

39

GRAND ROYAL CLOVER CLUB

2 jiggers Dry Gin
1 Tablespoon Grenadine
Juice of ½ Lemon
1 Egg

Shake with ice and strain.

GRAPEFRUIT

2 jiggers Dry Gin
1 jigger Grapefruit Juice

Shake with ice and strain.

GRAPE VINE

1 jigger Dry Gin
½ jigger Grape Juice
½ jigger Lemon Juice
1 Dash Grenadine

Stir with ice and strain.

GRASSHOPPER

½ jigger White Creme de Cacao
½ jigger Green Creme de Menthe
½ jigger Cream

Shake w i t h cracked ice. Strain.

GREAT SECRET

2 jiggers Dry Gin
1 jigger Lillet
1 Dash Angostura Bitters

Stir with ice and strain. Serve with twist of Orange Peel.

GREEN DRAGON NO. 2

1 jigger Green Chartreuse
1 jigger Brandy

Stir w i t h shaved ice and strain.

GREEN DRAGON SPECIAL

1 jigger Creme de Menthe
2 jiggers Dry Gin
½ jigger Kummel
½ jigger Lemon Juice
4 Dashes Peach Bitters

Shake with ice and strain.

GRENADINE FIZZ

2 jiggers Gin
2 Teaspoons Grenadine
Juice of ½ Lemon

Shake with ice and strain. Fill with Soda Water.

GRENADIER

2 jiggers Brandy
1 jigger Ginger Brandy
1 Dash Jamaica Ginger
1 Teaspoon Powdered Sugar

Stir with ice and strain.

GUNGA DIN

1½ jiggers Gin
½ jigger Dry Vermouth
1 Slice Pineapple
Juice of ¼ Orange

Shake with ice and strain.

HARROVIAN

2 jiggers Dry Gin
1 Teaspoon Orange Juice
1 Dash Lemon Juice
1 Dash Angostura Bitters

Stir with ice and strain.

HARRY'S

2 jiggers Dry Gin
1 jigger Sweet Vermouth
1 Dash Pernod
2 Sprigs Fresh Mint

Shake with ice and strain.
Serve with Mint Leaf.

H. AND H.

2 jiggers Dry Gin
1 jigger Lillet
2 Dashes Curacao

Stir with ice and strain. Serve
with a twist of Orange Peel.

HALF AND HALF
AMERICAN

Fill glass half full of Beer
and fill up with Porter.

HALF AND HALF
ENGLISH

Fill glass half full of Beer
and fill up with Ale.

HARRY'S PICK-ME-UP

2 jiggers Cognac
1 Teaspoon Grenadine
Juice of ½ Lemon

Shake with ice and strain.
Fill with iced Champagne.

HARVARD

1 jigger Brandy
1 jigger Sweet Vermouth
2 Dashes Angostura Bitters
1 Dash Sugar Syrup

Stir with ice and strain.

41

HASTY

1 jigger Gin
½ jigger Dry Vermouth
4 Dashes Grenadine
1 Dash Pernod

Shake with cracked ice and strain.

HAVE A HEART

1½ jiggers Dry Gin
½ jigger Swedish Punch
2 Dashes Grenadine
Juice of ½ Lime

Shake with shaved ice and strain. Serve with a wedge of Pineapple and a Cherry.

HAVANA STANDARD

1 jigger Light Rum
2/3 jigger Pineapple Juice
¼ jigger Lemon Juice

Shake with ice and strain.

HAVANA CLUB

1 jigger Gold Label Rum
½ jigger Dry Vermouth

Stir with ice and strain.

HAWAII

1 jigger Gin
¼ jigger Pineapple Juice
1 Dash Orange Bitters

Shake with cracked ice and strain.

HAWAIIAN STANDARD

1 jigger Dry Gin
½ jigger Pineapple Juice
1 Dash Orange Bitters
1 Egg White

Shake with ice and strain.

HAWAIIAN NO. 2

1 jigger Gin
¼ jigger Orange Juice
¼ jigger Curacao

Shake with ice and strain.

HAWAIIAN COOLER

1½ jiggers Rye Whiskey

Add twist of orange peel and fill with cold soda water.

HIGHLAND COOLER

2 jiggers Scotch
2 Dashes Angostura Bitters
Juice of ½ Lemon
1 Teaspoon Powdered Sugar

Fill with cold ginger ale.

HIGHLAND FLING

1 jigger Scotch
1 Teaspoon Sugar

1¼ jiggers Milk

Shake w i t h ice. Strain and sprinkle nutmeg on top.

HOFFMAN HOUSE FIZZ

2 jiggers Dry Gin
Juice of ½ Lemon
1 Teaspoon Sugar
1 Teaspoon Cream
2 Dashes Maraschino

Shake with ice and strain. Fill with Soda Water.

HOLLAND HOUSE

2 jiggers Dry Gin
1 jigger Dry Vermouth
Juice of ¼ Lemon
1 Slice Pineapple
4 Dashes Maraschino

Stir with ice and strain.

HOMESTEAD

2 jiggers Dry Gin
1 jigger Sweet Vermouth
1 Slice Orange

Shake with ice and strain.

HONEYBEE

1½ jiggers Light Rum
1/3 jigger Lemon Juice
1 Tablespoon Honey

Shake with ice and strain.

HONOLULU LULU

1 jigger Gin
1 jigger Claristine or
  Benedictine
1 jigger Maraschino

Stir with ice and strain.

HOOP LA

1 jigger Brandy
1 jigger Lemon Juice
1 jigger Cointreau
1 jigger Lillet

Stir with ice and strain.

HOT RUM TODDY

1 jigger Jamaican Rum
1 Teaspoon Sugar or Simple
  Syrup
2 or 3 Cloves
1 Dash Cinnamon or small
  piece of Cinnamon Bark
1 Dash Ground Nutmeg
1 thin slice Lemon

Combine all ingredients except nutmeg in tall heavy glass. Fill with hot water and dust top with nutmeg.

43

"HOOTS MON"

1 jigger Scotch Whiskey
½ jigger Lillet
½ jigger Sweet Vermouth

Stir with ice and strain.

HOT BUTTERED RUM

2 jiggers Jamaican rum
1 scant Teaspoon Butter
1 Teaspoon Maple Syrup
Dash each of Cinnamon,
    Allspice and bitters
Slice of Lemon
4 jiggers of boiling water

Place butter in preheated ceramic mug or heavy glass. Leave spoon in mug. Add syrup, spices, lemon and rum. Mix. Pour in boiling water. Stir.

HOT DECK

1½ jiggers Whiskey
1 jigger Sweet Vermouth
1 Dash Jamaica Ginger

Shake with ice and strain.

HOT TODDY

1½ jigger Liquor
1 Teaspoon Sugar
Small Stick of Cinnamon
Slice of Lemon
4 Cloves

Fill mug 2/3 full of boiling water. Add sugar, cinnamon stock, lemon slice studded with cloves, Liquor. Stir Serve with a spoon.

HOT TOMODDY

Heat 3 ounces tomato juice with celery salt, Tabasco and ½" square of bay leaf. Pour into cup or mug. Add 1 jigger of vodka.

HOT WINE LEMONADE

1 jigger Red Wine
Juice of ½ or 1 Lemon
1½ Teaspoons Sugar
Twist of Lemon Peel

Combine Sugar, Juice and Wine in a hot tumbler or mug. Add Boiling Water and twist of Lemon Peel.

HOUSE STANDARD

1 jigger Tequila
2 jiggers Tomato Juice
2 Dashes Tabasco

Shake with cracked ice and strain. Serve with slice of Lemon.

HORSE'S NECK (SPIKED)

1 jigger Whiskey
1 jigger Lemon

Remove lemon peel in one long spiral piece, drape one end over edge of tall highball glass. Fill with ginger ale.

HULA-HULA

2 jiggers Dry Gin
1 jigger Orange Juice
1 Dash Curacao

Shake with ice and strain.

HOUSTON HURRICANE

1 jigger Whiskey
1 jigger Gin
1 jigger White Creme de Menthe
Juice of 1 Lemon

Shake with ice and strain.

IMPERIAL MARTINI

1 jigger Dry Gin
1 jigger Dry Vermouth
1 Dash Angostura Bitters
1 Dash Maraschino

Stir with ice and strain. Serve with Olive

ICHBIEN

3 jiggers Brandy
1 jigger Curacao
1 Egg Yolk
Milk as desired

Shake with ice and strain. Sprinkle with Nutmeg.

IDEAL

1 jigger Gin
½ jigger Sweet Vermouth
3 Dashes Maraschino
1 Tablespoon Grapefruit Juice

Shake with ice and strain.

IMPERIAL FIZZ

1 jigger Rye or Bourbon Whiskey
Juice of ½ Lemon
½ Teaspoon Sugar

Shake with ice and strain. Fill with chilled Champagne.

45

IMPERIAL HOTEL FIZZ

2 jiggers Whiskey
1 jigger Light Rum
4 Dashes Lemon Juice
Juice of ½ Lime

Shake with ice and strain.
Fill with Soda Water.

INCA

1 jigger Dry Gin
1 jigger Sherry
1 jigger Dry Vermouth
1 jigger Sweet Vermouth
1 Dash Orgeat Syrup
1 Dash Orange Bitters

Stir with ice and strain.

INCOME TAX

1 jigger Dry Gin
½ jigger Dry Vermouth
½ jigger Sweet Vermouth
1 Dash Angostura Bitters
Juice of ¼ Orange

Stir with ice and strain.

INK STREET

1 jigger Whiskey
½ jigger Orange Juice
½ jigger Lemon Juice

Shake with ice and strain.

IRISH

1 jigger Irish Whiskey
2 Dashes Pernod
2 Dashes Curacao
1 Dash Maraschino
1 Dash Angostura Bitters

Stir w i t h ice and strain.
Squeeze Orange Peel on top.

IRISH COOLER

1 jigger Whiskey
1 Long twist Lemon Peel

Fill with Soda Water

IRISH ELEGANCE

3 jiggers Jamaica Rum
1 jigger Brandy
1 Teaspoon Creme de
    Violette
1/3 jigger Pineapple Juice
Juice of 1 Lime

Blend with shaved ice.

ITALIAN

2 jiggers Sweet Vermouth
1 jigger Fernet Branca
2 Dashes Sugar Syrup
1 Dash Pernod

Stir with ice and strain.

JABBERWOCK

1 jigger Dry Gin
1 jigger Dry Sherry
1 jigger Dubonnet
2 Dashes Orange Bitters

Stir w i t h ice and strain. Squeeze Lemon Peel over top and serve with a Cherry.

JACK ROSE

1 jigger Applejack
½ jigger Grenadine
Juice of ½ Lime

Shake with ice and strain.

JACK SLOAT

1 jigger Dry Gin
2 Dashes Dry Vermouth
4 Dashes Sweet Vermouth
3 Slice Pineapple

Shake with ice and strain.

JACK WITHERS

1 jigger Dry Gin
1 jigger Dry Vermouth
1 jigger Sweet Vermouth
Juice of ½ Orange

Stir with ice and strain.

JACKSON STANDARD

1½ jiggers Dry Gin
1½ jiggers Dubonnet
2 Dashes Orange Bitters

Stir with ice and strain.

JAMAICA GINGER

2 jiggers Jamaica Rum
1 jigger Grenadine
3 Dashes Maraschino
3 Dashes Curacao
1 Dash Angostura Bitters

Shake with ice and strain.

JAMAICAN

1 jigger Jamaican Rum
1 jigger Coffee Liqueur
1 jigger Lime Juice
Dash of Bitters

Shake with cracked ice. Pour unstrained into tall glass fill with 7-Up.

JANET STANDARD

2 jiggers Brandy
1 Dash Angostura Bitters
1 Teaspoon Orgeat Syrup

Place cube of ice in cocktail glass and add ingredients. Stir and s e r v e with twist of Lemon Peel.

47

JAVA COOLER

1 jigger Gin
Juice of ½ Lime
3 Dashes Bitters
Quinine Water

Place ice cubes in highball glass. Add juice of ½ lime, bitters and Gin. Fill with quinine water. Stir.

JOBURG

1 jigger Light Rum
1 jigger Dubonnet
4 Dashes Orange Bitters

Stir with ice and strain. Serve with twist of Lemon Peel.

JUDGE JR.

1 jigger Dry Gin
1 jigger Light Rum
1 jigger Lemon Juice
1-2 Dashes Grenadine

Shake with ice and strain.

JUDGETTE

1 jigger Dry Gin
1 jigger Peach Brandy
1 jigger Dry Vermouth
1 Dash Lime Juice

Stir with ice and strain.

KANGAROO COCKTAIL

1½ jigger Vodka
1 jigger Dry Vermouth

Stir with cracked ice. Strain Serve with twist of lemon peel.

KINA

1 jigger Dry Gin
½ jigger Sweet Vermouth
½ jigger Lillet

Stir with ice and strain.

KING COLE

1 jigger Bourbon Whiskey
1 Dash Fernet Branca
2 Dashes Sugar Syrup
1 Slice Orange
1 Slice Pineapple
1 Lump ice

Mix well.

KING'S PEG

One piece of ice in a large wine glass. Add 1 jigger Brandy fill with iced Champagne.

KITCHEN SINK

1 jigger Rye Whiskey
1 jigger Gin
1 jigger Lemon Juice
1 jigger Orange Juice
1 Egg
1 Teaspoon Apricot
   Brandy
½ Teaspoon Powdered Sugar

Shake with ice and strain.

KINGSTON

1 jigger Sugar Syrup
2 jiggers Lime or Lemon Juice
3 jiggers Gin
4 jiggers Jamaica Rum

Shake with cracked or crushed ice.

KLONDIKE COOLER

1 jigger Whiskey
Rind of 1 Orange
Juice of 1 Orange
Ginger Ale

Place ice cubes and whole orange rind in highball glass. Add orange juice and liquor. Stir. Fill with ginger ale.

KNICKERBOCKER

2 jiggers Dry Gin
1 jigger Dry Vermouth
1 Dash Sweet Vermouth

Stir with ice and strain. Squeeze Lemon Peel over top.

KNOCKOUT

1 jigger Gin
1 jigger Dry Vermouth
1 jigger Anesone or
   Abisante
1 Teaspoon White Creme de
   Menthe

Stir with ice and strain. Serve with mint leaves.

KNICKERBEIN

1 jigger Maraschino
1 jigger Grenadine
1 Egg Yolk
1 jigger Brandy

Shake with ice and strain.

KUP'S INDISPENSABLE

2 jiggers Dry Vermouth
4 jiggers Dry Gin
1 jigger Sweet Vermouth
1 Dash Angostura Bitters

Stir with ice and strain. Serve with twist of Orange Peel.

49

LADY BE GOOD

1 jigger Brandy
½ jigger White Creme de Menthe
½ jigger Sweet Vermouth

Shake with cracked ice and strain.

LADY FINGER

1 jigger Dry Gin
½ jigger Kirsch
½ jigger Cherry Brandy

Stir with ice and strain.

LADIES' COCKTAIL

1 jigger Whiskey
2 Dashes Abisante or Anesone
3 Dashes Anisette
1 Dash Bitters

Stir with ice and strain. Serve with piece of pineapple.

LAST ROUND

1 jigger Dry Gin
1 jigger Dry Vermouth
2 Dashes Brandy
2 Dashes Pernod

Stir with ice and strain.

LATIN MANHATTAN

1 jigger Rum
1 jigger Dry Vermouth
1 jigger Sweet Vermouth
2 Dashes Bitters

Pour in mixing glass. Fill with cracked ice. Stir and strain. Add twist of lemon peel and serve

LAURA'S THEME

1½ jigger Vodka
1 jigger Cherry Brandy
½ jigger Passion Fruit Nectar

Stir with ice. Strain

LAWHILL

2 jiggers Rye Whiskey
1 jigger Dry Vermouth
1 Dash Pernod
1 Dash Maraschino
1 Dash Angostura Bitters

Stir with ice and strain.

LAYER CAKE

1 jigger Creme de Cacao
1 jigger Apricot Brandy
1 jigger Cream

Pour carefully so that ingredients do not mix. Place Cherry on top. Chill mixture in glass.

LEILANI TIKI STANDARD

1 jigger Hawaiian Rum
Juice of ½ Lime
2 Dashes Grenadine
2 jiggers of Soda

Shake with ice and pour into Mug or tall glass. Garnish with fruit.

LEO SPECIAL

1 jigger Gin
½ jigger Lime Juice
½ jigger Triple Sec
2 Dashes Anesone or
    Abisante

Stir with ice and strain.

LIEBFRAUMILCH

1 jigger Creme de Cacao
1 jigger Cream
Juice of 1 Lime

Shake with ice and strain.

LITTLE DEVIL

1 jigger Dry Gin
1 jigger Light Rum
½ jigger Cointreau
½ jigger Lemon Juice

Stir with ice and strain.

LOCH LOMOND

1 jigger Scotch
3 Dashes Bitters
1 Teaspoon Sugar

Shake with ice. Serve in Old Fashioned glass.

LONDON

2 jiggers Dry Gin
2 Dashes Maraschino
2 Dashes Sugar Syrup
2 Dashes Orange Bitters

Stir with ice and strain. Serve with twist of Lemon Peel.

LONE TREE

1 jigger Dry Gin
1 jigger Sweet Vermouth
1 jigger Dry Vermouth
2 Dashes Orange Bitters

Stir with ice and strain. Serve with Cherry.

51

LORD SUFFOLK

4 jiggers Dry Gin
1 jigger Cointreau
1 jigger Sweet Vermouth
1 jigger Maraschino

Stir with ice and strain. Serve
with twist of Lemon Peel.

LOUD SPEAKER

3 jiggers Dry Gin
3 jiggers Brandy
1 jigger Cointreau
1 jigger Lemon Juice

Stir with ice and strain.

LOVE

1 jigger Sloe Gin
1 Egg White
2 Dashes Lemon Juice
2 Dashes Raspberry Syrup

Shake with ice and strain.

LOVER'S DELIGHT

1 jigger Cointreau
1 jigger Forbidden Fruit
1 jigger Brandy

LUIGI

1 jigger Dry Gin
1 jigger Dry Vermouth
Juice of ½ Tangerine
1 Dash Cointreau
1 Teaspoon Grenadine

Stir with ice and strain. Serve
with twist of Lemon Peel.

LUTKINS SPECIAL

1 jigger Dry Gin
1 jigger Dry Vermouth
2 Dashes Apricot Brandy
2 Dashes Orange Juice

Stir with ice and strain.

MABEL SPECIAL

1 jigger Sloe Gin
1 jigger Swedish Punch
Juice of ½ Lime

Shake with ice and strain.

MAGNOLIA BLOSSOM

1 jigger Gin
½ jigger Cream
½ jigger Lemon Juice
1 Dash Grenadine

Shake with ice and strain.

MAI TAI SPECIAL

2 jiggers Rum
Juice of 1 Lime
1 Dash Orange Curacao
2 Dashes Orgeat Syrup

Pour into large old fashioned glass; add a squeezed half lime shell; stir. Fill with shaved ice; garnish with pineapple and mint.

MAIDEN'S BLUSH

1 jigger Gin
4 Dashes Curacao
4 Dashes Grenadine
2 Dashes Lemon Juice

Shake with ice and strain

MAIDEN'S PRAYER

1 jigger Gin
1 jigger Triple Sec
1/3 jigger Lemon Juice
½ Teaspoon Orange Juice

Stir with ice and strain.

MANHATTAN STANDARD DRY

1 jigger French Vermouth
1 jiggers Whiskey
1 Dash Angostura

MAI-TAI

1 jigger Puerto Rican Rum
½ jigger Curacao or Triple Sec
½ jigger Lime Juice
½ Teaspoon Falernum

Pour into tall glass filled with shaved ice. Stir briskly.

MAMIE TAYLOR

1 jigger Scotch
Juice of ½ Lime
Ginger Ale

Squeeze lime into highball glass. Add ice cubes. Fill with ginger ale.

MANYANN

1 jigger Dry Gin
1 jigger Dubonnet
2 Dashes Curacao
Juice of 1 Lemon

Shake with ice and strain.

PERFECT MANHATTAN

1 jigger Bourbon
¼ jigger dry Vermouth
¼ jigger sweet Vermouth
1 Dash Bitters

Stir with ice and strain. Garnish with cherry.

MANHATTAN

1 jigger Whiskey
1/3 jigger Sweet Vermouth
1 Dash Bitters

Stir with ice and strain. Serve with cherry.

MR. MANHATTAN

2 jiggers Dry Gin
4 Dashes Orange Juice
1 Dash Lemon Juice
4 Crushed Mint Leaves
1 Lump Sugar moistened with water

Shake with ice and strain.

MANHATTAN DE LUXE

1 jigger Cina
1 jigger Cinzano Italian Vermouth
4 jiggers Bonded Whiskey
1 Dash Angostura to each drink

Stir in a bar glass with large cubes of ice and pour into chilled cocktail glasses. Add a maraschino cherry.

MARGUERITE'S STANDARD

2 jiggers Gin
1 jiggery Dry Vermouth
1 Dash Orange Bitters
1 Twist Orange Peel

Stir with ice and strain. Serve with a Cherry.

MARGARITA

1 jigger Tequila
½ jigger Triple Sec or Cointreau
½ jigger Lime Juice

Shake with cracked ice and strain into chilled cocktail glass frosted with salt.

MARNY

2 jiggers Dry Gin
1 jigger Grand Marnier

Stir with ice and strain. Serve with a Cherry

MARIACHI GRINGO

1 jigger Mariachi Tequila
4 jiggers Tomato Juice
½ Lime squeezed and dropped into glass.

Serve in glass filled with ice cubes. A dash of Tabasco.

MARTINI STANDARD DRY

4 jiggers Dry Gin
1 jigger Dry Vermouth

Stir with ice and strain.

100% DRY MARTINI

1 jigger Gin
1/3 jigger Dry Vermouth

Stir with ice and strain. Serve with twist of lemon peel or olive.

MARTINI (MEDIUM)

2 jiggers Dry Gin
1 jigger Dry Vermouth

Stir with ice and strain. Serve with twist of Lemon Peel or an Olive.

PERFECT MARTINI

1 jigger Gin
¼ jigger Dry Vermouth
¼ jigger Sweet Italian Vermouth

Stir with ice cubes and strain into cocktail glass.

SWEET MARTINI

1 jigger Gin
½ jigger Sweet Italian Vermouth
Dash Orange Bitters

Stir with ice cubes and strain.

MARTINI DE LUXE (GIBSON)

1 jigger Lillet Vermouth
6 jiggers imported English Gin

Stir in pitcher with cubes of ice and pour. Twist lemon peel over the top.

MARTINI-ON-THE-ROCKS

Pack an Old-Fashioned glass loosely with ice. Fill with Dry Gin and add a few dashes Dry Vermouth. Stir.

MARY PICKFORD

2 jiggers Rum
¾ jigger of Pineapple Juice
3 Dashes of Grenadine

Shake with cracked ice and strain into cocktail glass.

MATADOR

1 jigger Tequila
2 jiggers Pineapple Juice
½ jigger Lime Juice

Shake with crushed ice.

MARVEL

2 jiggers Jamaica Rum
½ jigger Grenadine
½ jigger Sirop de Citron

Shake with ice and strain.

MASTER OF THE HOUNDS

1 jigger Whiskey
½ jigger Cherry Brandy
2 Dashes Bitters

Stir with ice and strain.

MAURICE

1 jigger Gin
½ jigger Sweet Vermouth
½ jigger Dry Vermouth
Juice of ¼ Orange
1 Dash Bitters

Stir with ice and strain.

MERRY WIDOW COCKTAIL

1 jigger Cherry Brandy
1 jigger Maraschino

Shake with ice. Serve with Cherry.

MELBA

½ jigger Light Rum
2 Dashes Pernod
½ jigger Swedish Punch
Juice of ½ Lime
2 Dashes Grenadine

Shake with ice and strain.

MIAMI

1 jigger Light Rum
½ jigger White Creme de Menthe
2 or 3 Dashes Lemon Juice

Shake with ice and strain.

MIAMI BEACH STANDARD

1 jigger Rum
1/3 jigger Triple Sec
1 Dash Lime Juice

Shake with ice and strain.

MICKEY WALKER

1 jigger Scotch
½ jigger Sweet Vermouth
1 Dash Lemon Juice
1 Dash Grenadine

Shake with ice and strain.

MILK PUNCH

1 jigger Whiskey
1 Teaspoon Fine Granulated
   Sugar
4 oz. Milk

Shake with ice. Strain. Dust
nutmeg on top.

MILLION

1 jiggers Jamaica Rum
1 jigger Lime Juice
½ Teaspoon Powdered Sugar
1 Dash Angostura Bitters

Shake with shaved ice and
strain. Serve with a Cherry.

MILLIONAIRE

1 jigger Bourbon or Rye
½ jigger Curacao
1 Dash Grean

1 Dash Grenadine
White of 1 Egg

Shake and strain.

MILLIONAIRE NO. 2

1 jigger Jamaica Rum
1 jigger Apricot Brandy
1 jigger Sloe Gin
1 Dash Grenadine
Juice of 1 Lime

Shake with ice and strain.

MILLIONAIRE NO. 3

1 jigger Bourbon
1/3 jigger Curacao
1 Egg White
1 Dash Grenadine

Shake with shaved ice and
strain.

MINNEHAHA

1 jigger Gin
½ jigger Dry Vermouth
½ jigger Sweet Vermouth
Juice of ¼ Orange

Shake well with ice. Strain
into cocktail glass.

MINT COOLER

2 jiggers Scotch Whiskey, 3
dashes White Creme de
Menthe. Fill with Soda
Water.

MINT JULEP (COBB'S)

1½ jiggers Whiskey
4 Sprigs Fresh Mint
1 Small Lump Sugar

Dissolve sugar in ½ oz. water and crush 3 sprigs mint in large highball glass. Rub inside then discard mint. Fill glass with crushed ice. Add Liquor and sugar water. Do not stir. Garnish with remaining fresh mint.

MINT SMASH

1 jigger Whiskey
2 Sprigs Fresh Mint
1 Teaspoon Sugar
Soda

Crush mint and sugar in highball glass with a few drops of water. Add half a glass of shaved ice, then liquor.

MISSISSIPPI MULE

4 jiggers Dry Gin
1 jigger Lemon Juice
1 jigger Creme de Cassis

MODERN NO. 1

2 jiggers Sloe Gin
1 jigger Scotch Whiskey
1 Dash Pernod
1 Dash Orange Bitters
1 Dash Grenadine
Shake with ice and strain.

58

MODERN NO. 2

2 jiggers Scotch Whiskey
1 Dash Lemon Juice
1 Dash Pernod
2 Dashes Jamaica Rum
1 Dash Orange Bitters

Stir with ice, strain and serve with a cherry.

MODERN LEMONADE

1 jigger Sherry
1 jigger Sloe Gin
2 Tablespoons Powdered Sugar
Juice of 1 Lemon

Stir with ice and strain. Add twist of Lemon Peel and fill with Soda Water.

MONTE CARLO

1 jigger Bourbon or Rye
½ jigger Benedictine
2 Dashes Bitters

Shake with cracked ice and strain.

MORNING GLORY

2 jiggers Whiskey
2 jiggers Brandy
1 Dash Pernod
2 Dashes Bitters
2 Dashes Curacao
3 Dashes Sugar Syrup
1 Twist Lemon Peel

Stir with 2 cubes ice. Remove ice. Fill glass with Soda Water and stir with a teaspoon c o a t e d with powdered sugar.

MOONLIGHT

1 jiggers Calvados or
    Applejack
Juice of 1 Lemon
1½ Teaspoons Sugar

Shake with shaved ice and strain. Fill with Soda Water.

MORNING GLORY FIZZ

1 jigger Whiskey
1 jigger Bitters
Juice of ½ Lime
½ jigger Abisante or
    Anesone
White of 1 Egg
½ Teaspoon Fine
    Granulated Sugar

Shake with ice. Strain into a highball glass. Fill with soda.

MOSCOW MULE

2 jiggers Vodka
Ginger Beer
1 Slice Lime

Serve over ice in glass, brass or copper mug.

MOUNTAIN

2 jiggers Rye Whiskey
½ jigger Lemon Juice
½ jigger Dry Vermouth
½ jigger Sweet Vermouth
1 Egg White

Shake with ice and strain.

MY OWN PASSION

½ jigger Passion-Fruit Nectar
1 jigger Lime Juice
4 jiggers White Label Cuban
    Rum

Shake w i t h crushed ice. Strain.

NAPOLEON

2 jiggers Dry Gin
1 Dash Dubonnet
1 Dash Curacao
1 Dash Fernet Branca

Stir w i t h ice and strain. Squeeze Lemon Peel over top.

NAPOLI

1 jigger Campari
1 jigger Vodka
½ jigger Dry Vermouth
1/3 jigger Sweet Vermouth

Pour over cracked ice in a tall glass and stir. Fill with soda and stir again. Top with twist of orange peel.

NEW ORLEANS

1 jigger Bourbon
1 Dash Orange Bitters
2 Dashes Angostura Bitters
1 Dash Anisette
2 Dashes Pernod
½ Lump Sugar

Stir with ice and strain. Serve with twist of Lemon Peel.

NEW ORLEANS STANDARD FIZZ

1 jigger Gin
½ jigger Cream
1 Teaspoon Sugar or
    Simple Syrup
Juice of ½ Lime and ½
    Lemon
1 Egg White
Soda Water

Shake well with cracked ice. Strain and add 2 ounces of Soda and 3 dashes of Orange Flower Water.

NEGRONI

1 jigger Campari
1 jigger Gin
1 jigger Italian Vermouth

Stir with ice and strain. Twist of lemon peel and drop in glass.

NEWBURY

1 jigger Gin
1 jigger Sweet Vermouth
3 Dashes Curacao
1 Twist Lemon Peel
1 Twist Orange Peel

Stir with ice and strain.

NEWTON'S SPECIAL

3 jiggers Brandy
1 jigger Cointreau
1 Dash Angostura Bitters

Stir with ice and strain.

NEW YORK COCKTAIL

1 jigger Whiskey
½ Teaspoon Powdered Sugar
1 Dash Grenadine
Juice of ½ Lime

Shake w i t h ice. Strain.
Decorate with t w i s t of
orange peel.

NIGHT CAP

1 jigger Brandy
1 jigger Curacao
1 jigger Anisette
1 Egg Yolk

Shake with ice and strain.

NINETEEN

2 jiggers Dry Vermouth
½ jigger Dry Gin
½ jigger Kirsch
1 Dash Pernod
4 Dashes Sugar Syrup

Stir with ice and strain.

NINETEEN-TWENTY

2 jiggers Dry Gin
½ jigger Dry Vermouth
½ jigger Kirsch
1 Dash Orange Bitters
1 Teaspoon Groseille
   Syrup

Shake with ice and strain.

NONE BUT THE BRAVE

2 jiggers Brandy
1 jigger Pimento Dram
1 Teaspoon Powdered Sugar
1 Dash of Jamaica Ginger
1 Dash Lemon Juice

Shake with ice and strain.

ODD McINTYRE

½ jigger Brandy
½ jigger Cointreau
½ jigger Lillet
½ jigger Lemon Juice

Stir with ice and strain.

OLD FASHIONED

2 jiggers Whiskey
1 Small Lump Sugar
1 Dash Bitters

Muddle sugar in Old Fash-
ioned glass with spoonful of
water. Add ice, bitters, liquor. Garnish with cherry,
orange slice, and twist of
lemon peel as desired.

OLD-FASHIONED GIN

1½ jiggers Dry Gin
1 Slice Lemon Peel
½ Piece Lump Sugar
1 Dash Angostura Bitters

Place Sugar in bottom of Old-Fashioned g l a s s and sprinkle with Bitters. Add Lemon and ice cubes. Fill with Gin.

OLD ETONIAN

1 jigger Dry Gin
1 jigger Lillet
2 Dashes Orange Bitters
2 Dashes Creme de Noyau

Stir with ice and strain. Serve with twist of Orange Peel

OH, HENRY!

1 jigger Whiskey
1 jigger Benedictine
1 jigger Ginger Ale

Stir with ice and strain.

OLD TIME APPETIZER

½ jigger Rye or Bourbon
½ jigger Dubonnet
2 Dashes Curacao
2 Dashes Pernod
1 Slice Orange
1 Slice Pineapple
1 Twist Lemon Peel
1 Dash Peychaud's Bitters

Add ice cubes, and serve

OLD PEPPER

1 jigger Whiskey
Juice of ½ Lemon
1 Teaspoon Worcestershire
1 Teaspoon Chili Sauce or
1 Tablespoon Tomato
  Juice
2 or 3 Dashes Angostura
1 Dash Tabasco

OSTEND FIZZ

1 jigger Creme de Cassis
1 jigger Kirsch

Shake w i t h ice and strain. Fill with Soda Water.

ONE EXCITING NIGHT

1 jigger Gin
½ jigger Dry Vermouth
½ jigger Sweet Vermouth
1 Dash Orange Juice

Dip rim in lemon juice then sugar. Shake ingredients with ice. Strain into the frosted glass. Add twist of lemon peel.

OPENING

2 jiggers Whiskey
1 jigger Sweet Vermouth
½ jigger Grenadine

Stir with ice and strain.

ORANGE FIZZ NO. 2

2 jiggers Dry Gin
Juice of ½ Orange
Juice of ½ Lime
Juice of ¼ Lemon

Shake w e l l with ice and
strain into glass.   Fill up
with Soda Water.

ORANGE BLOOM

½ jigger Dry Gin
¼ jigger Sweet Vermouth
¼ jigger Cointreau

Stir with ice and strain. Serve
with a Cherry.

ORANGE BLOSSOM

2 jiggers Gin
1 jigger Orange Juice

Stir well with cracked ice
and strain into cocktail glass.

OPPENHEIM

½ jigger Bourbon
¼ jigger Grenadine
¼ jigger Sweet Vermouth

Stir with ice and strain.

PADDY

1 jigger Whiskey
1 jigger Sweet Vermouth
1 Dash Bitters

Stir with ice and strain.

PALISADES COCKTAIL

1 jigger Gin
1 jigger Cider
2 Dashes Bitters

Shake w i t h cracked ice.
Strain into cocktail glass.

PALL MALL

½ jigger English Gin
½ jigger Dry Vermouth
½ jigger Sweet Vermouth
1 Teaspoon White Creme de
    Menthe
1 Dash Orange Bitters

Stir with ice and strain.

PALMER COCKTAIL

1 jigger Bourbon
1 Dash Bitters
1 Dash Lemon Juice

Stir with ice and strain.

63

PANTOMIME

1 jigger Dry Vermouth
1 Egg White
1 Dash Grenadine
1 Dash Orgeat Syrup

Shake with ice and strain.

PARADISE

1 jigger Gin
1 jigger Apricot Brandy
1 jigger Orange or Lemon
   Juice

Stir with ice and strain.

PARISIAN

½ jigger Dry Gin
½ jigger Dry Vermoth
½ jigger Creme de Cassis

Stir with ice and strain.

PARK AVENUE

1 jigger Italian Vermouth
2 jiggers Pineapple Juice
4 jiggers Gin
2 Dashes Curacao

Shake with cracked ice.

PAULINE

1 jigger Rum
1 jigger Sweetened Lemon
   Juice
1 Dash Pernod
1 Grating of Nutmeg

Shake with ice and strain.

PINKY

1 jigger Dry Gin
1 jigger Grenadine
1 Egg White

Shake with cracked ice and
strain.

PEACH BLOW FIZZ

2 jiggers Dry Gin
2/3 jigger Cream
1 Teaspoon Powdered Sugar
4 Mashed Strawberries
Juice of ½ Lemon
Juice of ½ Lime

Shake with ice and strain.
Fill with Soda Water.

PERPETUAL

1 jigger Sweet Vermouth
1 jigger Dry Vermouth
4 Dashes Creme d'Yvette
2 Dashes Creme de Cacao

Stir with ice and strain.

Pi

PICK-UP

½ jigger Rye Whiskey
¼ jigger Fernet Branca
3 Dashes Pernod
1 Slice Lemon

Stir gently with a little ice and strain into glass.

PILGRIM

1 jigger New England Rum
1 Teaspoon Grenadine
Juice of ½ Lime or
 Lemon

Shake with ice and strain.

PICON

1 jigger Amer Picon
1 jigger Dry Vermouth

Stir with ice and strain.

PIMM'S CUP

1 jigger Pimm's No. 1
1 slice Lemon
7-Up (or other Lemon-
 flavored Soda)
Slice of Cucumber

Pour Pimm's over ice cubes in tall glass. Add lemon slice. Fill with 7-Up and garnish with cucumber slice.

PINEAPPLE FIZZ

2 jiggers Light Rum
½ Tablespoon Powdered
 Sugar
2 Tablespoons Pineapple
 Juice
1 Dash Lime Juice

Shake with ice and strain. Fill with Soda Water.

PINK LADY

1 jigger Gin
½ jigger Grenadine
White of One Egg

Shake with cracked ice and strain.

PINK LADY NO. 1

1 jigger Dry Gin
1 jigger Apple Brandy
1 Tablespoon Grenadine
1 jigger Lemon Juice
1 Egg White

Shake with ice and strain.

PINK LADY NO. 2

1 jigger Gin
½ jigger Lemon Juice
1 Tablespoon Grenadine
1 Egg White

Shake and pour.

65

PINK ROSE

2/3 jigger Dry Gin
1 Teaspoon Grenadine
1 Teaspoon Lemon Juice
1 Teaspoon Cream
1 Egg White

Shake with ice and strain.

PIRATE STANDARD

2 jiggers Dark Rum
1 jigger Vermouth
1 Dash Angostura Bitters

Stir with ice and strain.

PISCO PUNCH

2 jiggers Brandy
1 Teaspoon Lemon Juice
1 Teaspoon Pineapple Juice
Cube Pineapple

Put in tall glass over ice cubes and f i l l with cold water. Stir well.

PLANTER'S PUNCH

2 jiggers Leilani Rum
½ jigger Lime Juice
1 Teaspoon Sugar

Shake Rum, lime juice and sugar. Pour over cracked ice. Garnish with cherry and half slices of lemon, orange, and pineapple.

PLANTER'S NO. 1

1 jigger Rum
1 jigger Orange Juice
1 Dash Lemon Juice

Shake w e l l with ice and strain into glass.

PLANTER'S NO. 2

1 jigger Dark Rum
½ jigger Lemon Juice
½ jigger Sugar Syrup

Stir well with ice and strain into glass.

PLATINUM BLONDE

1 jigger Light Rum
1 jigger Cointreau
1/3 jigger Cream

Shake with ice and strain.

POLLYANNA

1 jigger Gin
1/3 jigger Grenadine
1/3 jigger Sweet Vermouth
3 Slices Orange
3 Slices Pineapple

Muddle orange and pineapple in bottom of shaker. Add ice and strain.

POLLY'S SPECIAL

1 jigger Scotch Whiskey
½ jigger Unsweetened
  Grapefruit Juice
¼ jigger Curacao

Shake with ice and strain.

POLO

1 jigger Gin
½ jigger Grapefruit Juice
½ jigger Orange Juice

Shake with cracked ice and strain.

PORT STANDARD

2 jiggers Port
1 Dash Brandy

Stir w i t h ice and strain. Squeeze Orange Peel over top.

PORT NO. 2

2 jiggers Port
2 Dashes Curacao
1 Dash Orange Bitters
1 Dash Angostura Bitters

Stir with ice and strain.

PORT SANGAREE

2 jiggers Port
1 jigger Water
½ Teaspoon Powdered Sugar

Stir with ice and strain.

POUSSE CAFE

1/3 jigger Grenadine
1/3 jigger Maraschino
1/3 jigger Green Creme de
  Menthe
1/3 jigger Creme de Violette
1/3 jigger Chartreuse
1/3 jigger Brandy

Slowly pour, one by one, into a cordial glass, to form layers.

PRINCE CHARLIE

½ jigger Drambuie
½ jigger Brandy
½ jigger Lemon Juice

Shake with cracked ice and strain.

67

PRINCESS MARY'S PRIDE

1 jigger Apple Brandy
½ jigger Dubonnet
½ jigger Dry Vermouth

Stir well with ice and strain into glass.

PRAIRIE OYSTER

½ jigger Cognac
1 Tablespoon Vinegar
1 Tablespoon Worcestershire
1 Teaspoon Catsup
1 Teaspoon Angostura

Prepare in serving glass without ice. Carefully add the yolk of an egg and a small dash of cayenne. Do not mix.

PRINCETON COCKTAIL

1 jigger Gin
1/3 jigger Port
2 Dashes Orange Bitters

Stir with ice. Strain into cocktail glass. Serve with a twist of lemon peel.

PRESIDENTE

2 jiggers Puerto Rican White Label Rum
¼ jigger Dry Vermouth
2 Dashes Grenadine

Shake with cracked ice and strain.

PURPLE BUNNY

1 jigger Cherry Brandy
1/3 jigger Creme de Cacao
2/3 jigger Cream

Shake with ice and strain.

QUEEN

1 jigger Dry Gin
½ jigger Sweet Vermouth
3 Slices Pineapple

Muddle Pineapple slices in shaker. Add other ingredients with ice. Stir well and strain.

QUEEN ELIZABETH NO. 1

1 jigger Dry Gin
½ jigger Cointreau
½ jigger Lemon Juice
1 Dash Pernod

Stir with ice and strain.

QUEEN ELIZABETH NO. 2

1 jigger Brandy
1 jigger Sweet Vermouth
1 Dash Curacao

Stir with ice and strain.

QUEEN ELIZABETH WINE

1 jigger Dry Vermouth
½ jigger Benedictine
½ jigger Lime or Lemon Juice

Stir with ice and strain.

QUEEN'S

1 jigger Dry Gin
½ jigger Dry Vermouth
½ jigger Sweet Vermouth
½ Slice Pineapple

Muddle the Pineapple in shaker. Add ice and other ingredients and stir. Strain.

QUELLE VIE

1 jigger Brandy
½ jigger Kummel

Stir with ice and strain.

QUICKIE

1 jigger Bourbon
1 jigger Light Rum
¼ jigger Triple Sec

Shake with cracked ice and strain.

RACQUET CLUB

1 jigger English Gin
½ jigger Dry Vermouth
1 Dash Orange Bitters

Stir with ice and strain.

RAIL SPLITTER

Juice of ½ Lemon
2/3 jigger Sugar Syrup

Pour into glass with ice and fill with Ginger Beer.

RAMOS FIZZ

1 jigger Gin
Juice of ½ Lemon
Juice of ½ Lime
1 jigger Cream
½ Teaspoon Sugar
White of 1 Egg

Shake well with crushed ice and strain.

RAY LONG

1½ jiggers Brandy
3/4 jigger Sweet Vermouth
4 Dashes Pernod
1 Dash Angostura Bitters

Stir with ice and strain.

RED BIRD SPECIAL

1 jigger Vodka
3 jiggers Tomato Juice

Pour into tall glass and fill with cold beer.

RED LIEON

2/3 jigger Grand Marnier
2/3 jigger Dry Gin
1/3 jigger Lemon Juice
1/3 jigger Orange Juice

Shake with ice and strain. Serve with twist of Lemon Peel.

69

RESOLUTE

1 jigger Dry Gin
½ jigger Apricot Brandy
½ jigger Lemon Juice

Stir with ice and strain.

RHETT BUTLER

1 jigger Southern Comfort
Juice of ¼ lime
Juice of ¼ lemon
1 Teaspoon Curacao
½ Teaspoon Sugar or Simple
  Syrup

Shake well with cracked ice
and strain.

ROMAN CANDLE

1 jigger Campari
1 jigger Cranberry Juice
Juice of ¼ Lemon

Pour over ice. Squeeze in
lemon juice and drop in rind
and stir.

ROB ROY

1 jigger Scotch
1 jigger Sweet Vermouth
2 Dashes Bitters

Stir with ice. Strain. Serve
with twist of lemon peel.

ROSE IN JUNE FIZZ

1 jigger Gin
1 jigger Framboise
Juice of 1 Orange
Juice of 2 Limes

Shake with ice and strain.
Add dashes of Soda Water.

ROSE NO. 3

1 jigger Kirsch
1 jigger Dry Vermouth
1 Teaspoon Grenadine

Stir with ice and strain.

ROSELYN

1 jigger Dry Gin
½ jigger Dry Vermouth
2 Dashes Grenadine

Stir with ice and strain.
Squeeze Lemon Peel over top.

ROSINGTON

1 jigger Dry Gin
½ jigger Sweet Vermouth

Stir with ice and strain. Squeeze
Orange Peel over top.

70

ROULETTE

1 jigger Apple Brandy
½ jigger Light Rum
½ jigger Swedish Punch

Stir with ice and strain.

ROYAL CLOVER CLUB

2 jiggers Gin
Juice of ½ Lemon
1 Tablespoon Grenadine
1 Egg Yolk

Shake well with ice and strain.

ROYAL NO. 1

1 jigger Gin
Juice of ½ Lemon
1 Egg
½ Teaspoon Powdered Sugar

Shake well with ice and strain.

ROYAL NO. 2

1 jigger Dry Gin
1 jigger Dry Vermouth
1 jigger Cherry Brandy

Stir with ice and strain.

ROYAL SMILE

1 jigger Dry Gin
1 jigger Grenadine
2 Dashes Lemon Juice

Stir with ice and strain
into glass.

RUM COLLINS

2 jiggers Rum
Juice of ½ Lemon
1 Teaspoon Sugar

Pour Rum in glass over ice.
Stir. Add soda, cherry, slice
of orange.

RUM COW
STANDARD

1 jigger Puerto Rican Rum
2 Drops Vanilla
1 Pinch Nutmeg
1 Dash Angostura Bitters
1 Cup Milk
1 Teaspoon Sugar

Shake with ice and pour.

RUM MANHATTAN

1 jigger Rum
1 jigger Sweet Vermouth
1 Dash Bitters

Stir in ice and strain.

RUM
OLD FASHIONED

2 jiggers Rum
1 Small Lump Sugar
1 Dash Bitters

Muddle sugar in glass with spoonful of water. Add ice, bitters, Rum. Garnish with cherry, o r a n g e slice, and twist of lemon peel. Add a splash of soda.

RUM SWIZZLE

2 jiggers Jamaican Rum
Juice of ½ Lime
1 Teaspoon Sugar or Simple
Syrup
Dash of Pernod
Dash of Bitters

Stir until chilled. Pour into tall glass of s h a v e d ice. Churn well with swizzle stick.

RUM ON THE ROCKS

Fill Old Fashioned glass with cracked ice, add Rum. Serve with lemon peel.

RUSSIAN

1 jigger Dry Gin
1 jigger Vodka
1 jigger Creme de Cacao

Stir with ice and strain.

RUM SOUR

2 jiggers Rum
Juice of 1 Lime
Sugar to taste

Shake well with shaved ice. Strain into sour glass. Add slice of orange and cherry.

RUSSELL HOUSE
(DOWN THE HATCH)

2 jiggers Rye Whiskey
3 Dashes Blackberry Brandy
2 Dashes Sugar Syrup
2 Dashes Orange Bitters

Stir with ice and strain.

SALTY DOG

2 jiggers gin
4 jiggers grapefruit juice

Fill tall glass almost full with shaved ice and pour in gin and juice. Add pinch of salt and stir well.

SALOME

½ jigger Gin
½ jigger Dry Vermouth
1 Tablespoon Sweet
    Vermouth

Stir with ice. Strain.

SAN JUAN COOLER

2 jiggers Puerto Rican rum
¼ jigger lemon juice
2 jiggers pineapple juice

Pour over ice cubes into tall glass and stir well. Fill with quinine water. Stir again lightly.

SANTIAGO

2 jiggers Rum
2 Dashes Grenadine
4 Dashes Lime Juice

Stir with ice. Strain.

SARATOGA FIZZ

1 jigger Bourbon
1/3 jigger Lemon Juice
1 Teaspoon Lime Juice
1 Teaspoon Sugar
1 Egg White

Shake with ice. Strain. Garnish with cherry.

SARATOGA NO. 1

2 jiggers Brandy
2 Dashes Maraschino
2 Dashes Angostura Bitters
¼ Slice Pineapple

Shake with ice and strain. Dash of Soda water.

SAUCY SUE

1 jigger Brandy
1 jigger Apple Brandy
1 Dash Apricot Brandy
1 Dash Pernod

Stir with ice and strain into glass. Squeeze Orange Peel over top.

SAVOY HOTEL

1 jigger Brandy
1 jigger Benedictine
1 jigger Creme de Cacao

Pour ingredients carefully do not mix.

SAZERAC

2 jiggers Bourbon
2 Dashes Anesone or
    Abisante
2 Dashes Bitters
1 Lump Sugar,
    dissolved in
    1 teaspoon water

Stir with ice. Strain. Twist lemon peel over top.

SAVOY SPECIAL

1 jigger Gin
2/3 jigger Dry Vermouth
2 Dashes Grenadine
1 Dash Anesone or Abisante

Stir with ice. Strain. Add lemon peel.

SCARLETT O'HARA

1½ jiggers Cranberry Juice
1 jigger Lime Juice
4 jiggers Southern Comfort

Shake with crushed ice.

SCOFF-LAW

1 jigger Rye Whiskey
1 jigger Dry Vermouth
½ jigger Lemon Juice
½ jigger Grenadine
1 Dash Orange Bitters

Stir with ice and strain.

SAXON

1 jigger Rum
2 Dashes Grenadine
1 Twist Orange Peel
Juice of ½ Lime

Shake with ice & strain.

SCREWDRIVER
STANDARD

1 jigger Vodka
Chilled Orange Juice

Place three ice cubes in a tall
glass. Add vodka and enough
orange juice to fill and stir.

SCOTCH-ON-THE-ROCKS

Fill Old-Fashioned glass with
ice cubes. Pour in Whiskey.

SCOTCH SIDE CAR

1 jigger Scotch Whiskey
½ jigger Cointreau
½ jigger Lemon Juice

Shake w e l l with ice and
strain.

SCOTCH SOUR

1 jigger Scotch
Juice of ½ Lemon
½ Teaspoon Sugar

Shake with ice. Garnish with
cherry and orange slices.

SELF—STARTER

4 jiggers Dry Gin
2 jiggers Lillet
1 jigger Apricot Brandy
2 Dashes Pernod

Stir with ice and strain.

SENSATION

3 jiggers Dry Gin
1 jigger Lemon Juice
3 Dashes Maraschino
3 Sprigs Fresh Mint

Shake with ice and strain.

SEPTEMBER MORN

1 jigger Rum
3 Dashes Grenadine
Juice of ½ Lime
1 Egg White

Shake with ice and strain.

SEVENTH REGIMENT

1 jigger Dry Gin
½ jigger Sweet Vermouth
2 Twists of Thin Lemon Peel

Stir with ice and strain.

SEVENTH HEAVEN

½ jigger Gin
½ jigger Sweet Vermouth
2 Dashes Maraschino
1 Dash Bitters

Stir with ice and strain. Add orange peel, cherry.

SEVENTH HEAVEN NO. 2

1½ jiggers Gin
½ jigger Marschino
1 Tablespoon Grapefruit
   Juice

Stir with ice and strain. Serve with a sprig of fresh Mint.

SEVILLA NO. 1

1 jigger Dark Rum
1 jigger Sweet Vermouth
1 Twist Orange Peel

Stir with ice and strain.

SEVILLA NO. 2

1 jigger Light Rum
1 jigger Port
1 Egg
½ Teaspoon Powdered Sugar

Shake with ice and strain.

SHARKY PUNCH

3 jiggers Apple Brandy
1 jigger Rye Whiskey
1 Teaspoon Sugar Syrup

Shake with ice and strain. Dash of Soda Water.

SHAMROCK—FRIENDLY SONS OF ST. PATRICK

1 jigger Irish Whiskey
1 jigger Dry Vermouth
3 Dashes Green
   Chartreuse
3 Dashes Green Creme de
   Menthe

Stir with ice and strain. Serve with Green Olive.

SHERRY COBBLER

Sherry
1 Teaspoon Sugar
1 Teaspoon Orange Juice

Fill highball glass 2/3 full of cracked ice. Add sugar and orange juice. Fill with Sherry. Stir. Decorate with orange slice.

76

SHERRY COCKTAIL

2 jiggers Dry Sherry,
   pre-chilled
1 jiggers Vermouth
   pre-chilled

Pour into cocktail glass. Stir
gently.

SIDE CAR

½ jigger Brandy
½ jigger Triple Sec or
   Cointreau
½ jigger Lemon or lime juice

Shake with cracked ice and
strain.

SINK OR SWIM

3 jiggers Brandy
1 jigger Sweet Vermouth
1 Dash Angostura Bitters

Stir well with ice and strain
into glass.

SHIP

1 jigger Sherry
¼ jigger Whiskey
2 Dashes Rum
2 Dashes Prune Syrup
2 Dashes Orange Bitters

Shake with ice and strain.

SILVER

1 jigger Dry Gin
1 jigger Dry Vermouth
2 Dashes Orange Bitters
2 Dashes Maraschino

Stir with ice and strain. Serve
with twist of Lemon Peel

SHRINER

½ jigger Sloe Gin
½ jigger Brandy
2 Dashes Sugar Syrup
2 Dashes Peychaud's
   Bitters

Stir with ice and strain. Serve
with a twist of Lemon Peel.

SILVER BULLET

1 jigger Dry Gin
1 jigger Kummel
¼ jigger Lemon Juice

Stir with ice and strain.

SILVER KING

1 jigger Gin
Juice of ½ lemon
2 Dashes Orange Bitters
2 Dashes Sugar Syrup
1 Egg White

Shake with ice and strain.

SLEDGE HAMMER

1 jigger Brandy
1 jigger Rum
1 jigger Apple Brandy
1 Dash Pernod

Shake with ice and strain.

SLOEBERRY

2 jiggers Sloe Gin
1 Dash Orange Bitters
1 Dash Angostura Bitters

Stir with ice and strain.

SLOE GIN NO. 1

1½ jiggers Sloe Gin
½ jigger Dry Vermouth

Stir with ice and strain.

SLOE GIN NO. 2

1½ jiggers Sloe Gin
2 Dashes Orange Bitters
2 Dashes Angostura Bitters

Shake w e l l with ice and
strain into glass.

SNOWBALL

1 jigger Gin
1/3 jigger White Creme
   de Menthe
½ jigger Anisette
½ jigger Cream

Shake with ice and strain.

SNYDER

2 Dashes Curacao
1 jigger Dry Gin
½ jigger Vermouth

Stir with ice and strain. Serve
with ice cube and twist of
Orange Peel.

SOCKO

1 jigger English Gin
½ jigger Dry Vermouth
2 Dashes Pernod

Shake with ice and strain.
Serve with a Pickled Pearl
Onion.

SONORA

1 jigger Bacardi Rum
1 jigger Calvados or
    Applejack

2 Dashes Apricot Brandy
1 Dash Lemon Juice

Stir with ice and strain.

SO-SO

1 jigger Dry Gin
1 jigger Sweet Vermouth
½ jigger Apple Brandy
½ jigger Grenadine

SOUR KISSES

2/3 jigger Dry Gin
1/3 jigger Dry Vermouth
1 Egg White

Shake w e l l with ice and strain into glass.

SOUTHERN BRIDE

2/3 jigger Dry Gin
1/3 jigger Grapefruit Juice
3 Dashes Maraschino

Shake w e l l with ice and strain into glass.

SOUTHERN GIN

2 jiggers Dry Gin
2 Dashes Orange Bitters
2 Dashes Curacao

Shake w e l l with ice and strain into glass. Serve with a twist of Lemon Peel.

SOUTHSIDE

2 jiggers Gin
Juice of ½ Lemon
½ Tablespoon Sugar
2 Sprigs of Fresh Mint

Shake w e l l with ice and strain into cocktail glass. Add a dash of soda.

SOUVENIR

1 jigger Whiskey
1 jigger Dry Vermouth
1 Orange Slice
1 Slice Orange

Stir well with ice.   Strain into cocktail glass.

SOVIET STANDARD

1 jigger French Vermouth
1 jigger Dry Sherry
6 jiggers Vodka

Stir with large ice cubes.

SPANISH TOWN

1 jigger Rum
2 Dashes Curacao

Shake shaved ice and strain.
Serve with a grating of Nutmeg.

SPECIAL ROUGH

½ jigger Applejack
½ jigger Brandy
1 Dash Pernod

Stir w i t h shaved ice and
strain into glass

ST. MARK

1 jigger Burrough's Beefeater
  Gin
1 jigger Dry Vermouth
½ jigger Cherry Brandy
½ jigger Groseille Syrup

Stir w e l l with ice and strain
into glass.

STANDARD LAW

2 jiggers Dry Sherry
1 jigger Dry Gin

Stir with ice and strain. A
twist of Lemon.

STAR NO. 1

1 jigger Applejack
1 jigger Sweet Vermouth
1 Dash Orange Bitters

Stir with cracked ice and
strain into glass.

STARS AND STRIPES

1 jigger Green Chartreuse
1 jigger Maraschino
1 jigger Creme de Cassis

Pour carefully into liqueur
glass so that ingredients do
not mix. Serve after dinner.

STRAWBERRY FIZZ

1 jigger Gin
4 Crushed Strawberries
½ Teaspoon Sugar
Juice of ½ Lemon

Shake w e l l with ice and
strain into glass. Fill up with
Soda Water.

STONE FENCE NO. 1

2 jiggers Applejack
1-2 Dashes Angostura
  Bitters

Place in tall glass with ice
and fill with Cider.

STUBBY COLLINS

1 jigger Gin
½ jigger Lemon Juice
1 Teaspoon Fine
  Granulated Sugar

Stir well wtih ice. Serve in Old Fashioned Glass.

SUMMER DELIGHT

Place 2 or 3 ice cubes in a large tumbler. Add the Juice of 1 Lime and ½ Jigger Raspberry Syrup. Fill up with Soda W a t e r and decorate with fruit as desired. Stir and serve.

SUMMER TIME

3 jiggers Gin
1 jigger Sirop de Citron

Stir with ice and strain. Fill up with Soda Water.

SUNSHINE NO. 1

2 jiggers Dry Gin
1 jigger Sweet Vermouth
1 Dash Angostura Bitters
1 Lump of Ice

Stir together and strain into glass. Squeeze Orange Peel over top.

SUNRISE STANDARD

1 jigger Mariachi Tequila
1/3 jigger Grenadine
Juice of ½ Lime

Shake with cracked ice and serve in a tall glass, filled with soda.

SWEET PATOOTIE

1 jigger Dry Gin
½ jigger Cointreau
½ jigger Orange Juice

Stir well with ice and strain into glass.

SWISS COCKTAIL

1 jigger Dubonnet
½ jigger Kirsch

Stir with ice. Strain into cocktail glass. Garnish with twist of orange peel.

SWIZZLES

2 jiggers Gin
Juice of 1 Lime
1 Dash Angostura Bitters
1 Teaspoon Sugar

Stir with swizzle stick until it foams. Add 1 lump of Ice.

81

T.N.T.

½ jigger Whiskey
½ jigger Anesone or
    Abisante

Shake well with ice. Strain
into cocktail glass.

TANGLEFOOT

1 jigger Light Rum
1 jigger Swedish Punch
½ jigger Orange Juice
½ jigger Lemon Juice

Shake with ice and strain.

TEMPTATION

1 jigger Bourbon or Rye
½ Teaspoon Curacao
½ Teaspoon Pernod
½ Teaspoon Dubonnet

Stir well with ice and strain
into cocktail glass. Decorate
with orange or lemon peel.

TEQUILA DAISY
FOR TWO

2½ jiggers Mariachi Tequila
½ jigger Lemon Juice
½ jigger Grenadine
½ jigger Club Soda

Shake all ingredients with
cracked ice and strain into
two chilled cocktail glasses.

TEQUILA STANDARD
MARTINI

2 jiggers Mariachi Tequila
½ jigger Dry Vermouth
Twist of orange or
    lemon peel

Stir with ice. Serve on rocks.
Garnish with twist.

TEXAS ABA FIZZ

1 jigger Gin
1 Dash Grenadine
Juice of ¼ Orange
Juice of ¼ Lemon

Shake w e l l with ice and
strain into glass. Fill up with
chilled Champagne.

THISTLE

2 jiggers Brandy
2 jiggers Green Creme de
  Menthe
1 Pinch Red Pepper

Shake Brandy and Creme de
Menthe and strain into glass.
Sprinkle Red Pepper on top.

THIRD DEGREE

2/3 jigger English Gin
1/3 jigger Dry Vermouth
4 Dashes Pernod

Stir well with ice and strain
into glass.

THREE STRIPES

1 jigger Gin
½ jigger Dry Vermouth
½ jigger Orange Juice

Shake well with cracked ice
and strain into cocktail glass.

THIRD RAIL STANDARD

1 jigger Brandy
1 jigger Calvados or Apple
  Brandy
1 jigger Light Rum
1 Dash Pernod

Shake with ice and strain.

THREE MILLER

2/3 jigger Brandy
1/3 jigger Light Rum
1 Dash Lemon Juice
1 Teaspoon Grenadine

Stir well with ice and strain.

THUNDER

2 jiggers Brandy
1 Teaspoon Sugar Syrup
1 Egg Yolk
1 Pinch Cayenne Pepper

Shake w e l l with ice and
strain into glass.

TIN WEDDING

¾ jigger Brandy
¾ jigger Dry Gin
¾ jigger Sweet Vermouth
2 Dashes Orange Bitters

Shake w e l l with ice and
strain into glass.

TINTON

2/3 jigger Applejack
1/3 jigger Port Wine

Stir well with ice and strain into glass.

TIPPERARY

¾ jigger Irish Whiskey
¾ jigger Green Chartreuse
¾ jigger Sweet Vermouth

Stir well with ice and strain into cocktail glass.

TOMATE

Place in a tumbler of highball glass with ice cubes 2 dashes Pernod and 1 teaspoon Grenadine. Fill with plain Water as desired.

TOM AND JERRY STANDARD

1 jigger Puerto Rican Rum
½ jigger Brandy or Cognac
1 Egg
1 Teaspoon Brown Sugar
¼ Teaspoon Allspice
Hot milk or water

Separate egg. Beat yolk with sugar and allspice. Gradually beat in liquors. Beat egg white. Fold into egg yolk mixture and pour into cup or mug. Add hot water or milk to fill.

TOM 'N' JERRY NO. 2

1 jigger Whiskey
1 Egg, separated
1 Teaspoon Sugar
Hot Water or Milk

Beat yolk and white separately, adding sugar to yolk. Mix. Put two tablespoonsful of batter in large mug. Add Whiskey. Fill with hot water or milk. Top with grated nutmeg. Brandy or rum may be added.

TOM COLLINS STANDARD

1 jigger Gin
1 jigger Lemon Juice
1 Teaspoon Sugar or Simple
    Syrup
Club Soda

TOREADOR

1 jigger Mariachi Tequila
1/3 jigger Creme de Cacao
1/3 jigger Sweet Cream

Shake w i t h cracked ice. Strain. Top with spoonful of whipped cream. Sprinkle with powdered cocoa.

TOVARICH

1 jigger Vodka
2/3 jigger Kummel
Juice of ½ Lime

Shake with cracked ice and strain.

TRILBY NO. 2

1 jigger Scotch Whiskey
1 jigger Sweet Vermouth
1 jigger Parfait Amour
    Liqueur
2 Dashes Orange Bitters
2 Dashes Pernod

Stir with ice and strain.

TRINIDAD

1 jigger Rum
Juice of ½ Lime
1 Teaspoon Powdered Sugar
3 Dashes Bitters

Shake well with ice. Strain into cocktail glass.

TURF

1 jigger Gin
½ jigger Dry Vermouth
2 Dashes Anisette
2 Dashes Marschino
2 Dashes Bitters

Shake with ice, strain.

TUXEDO

1 jigger Gin
½ jigger Medium Dry Sherry
1 Dash Bitters

Stir with ice and strain.

TUXEDO NO. 2

1 jigger Dry Gin
1 jigger Dry Vermouth
2 Dashes Orange Bitters
1 Dash Pernod
1 Dash Maraschino

Stir with ice and strain. Add a Cherry and squeeze Lemon Peel.

TWIN SIX

1 jigger Gin
½ jigger Sweet Vermouth
1 Dash Grenadine
3 Slices Orange
1 Egg White

Shake with ice and strain.

ULANDA

2 jiggers Dry Gin
1 jigger Cointreau
1 Dash Pernod

Stir with ice and strain.

UNION JACK

2/3 jigger Dry Gin
1/3 jigger Creme d'Yvette

Stir well with ice and strain
into glass.

UP IN THE AIR

1 jigger Dry Gin
1/3 jigger Lemon Juice
2 Teaspoons Maraschino

Shake well w i t h ice and
strain into glass.

UP-TO-DATE

1 jigger Whiskey
1 jigger Sherry
3 Dashes Bitters
2 Dashes Tiple Sec

Stir well with ice. Strain into
cocktail glass.

VALENCIA

2 jiggers Apricot Brandy
1 jigger Orange Juice
4 Dashes Orange Bitters

Stir well with ice and strain
into glass.   Fill with Champagne.

VAN

2 jiggers Dry Gin
1 jigger Dry Vermouth
2 Dashes Grand Marnier

Stir with ice and strain.

VANDERBILT HOTEL

3 jiggers Brandy
1 jigger Cherry Brandy
2 Dashes Angostura Bitters
2 Dashes Sugar Syrup

Stir with ice and strain.

VELOCITY

1 jigger Dry Gin
2 jiggers Sweet Vermouth
1 Slice Orange

Shake w e l l with ice and
strain into glass.

VERMOUTH NO. 1

2 jiggers Vermouth, Dry or
  Sweet
2 Dashes Angostura Bitters

Stir with ice and strain.

VERMOUTH NO. 2

1½ jiggers Sweet Vermouth
½ Teaspoon Curacao
1 Teaspoon Amer Picon
½ Teaspoon Powdered Sugar
1 Dash Angostura Bitters

Stir with ice and strain. Serve
with twist of Lemon Peel
and a Cherry.

VERMOUTH CASSIS

¾ jigger Creme de Cassis
1 jigger Dry Vermouth
Soda Water

Pour creme de cassis and vermouth into tall glass over ice.
Stir quickly, add soda water
to fill, stir once more.

VERMOUTH FRAPPE

1½ jiggers Sweet Vermouth
1 Dash Angostura Bitters

Stir w i t h shaved ice and
strain into glass.

VICTOR

1 jigger Dry Gin
1 jigger Brandy
½ jigger Sweet Vermouth

Stir well with ice and strain
into glass.

VIOLET FIZZ

1 jigger Dry Gin
1 Teaspoon Raspberry
  Syrup
1 Teaspoon Cream
Juice of ½ Lemon

Shake w e l l with ice and
strain into glass. Fill up with
Soda Water.

VODKA STANDARD

1 jigger Vodka
½ jigger Cherry Brandy
Juice of ½ Lemon or
  Lime

Shake w i t h ice and strain
into glass.

87

VODKA GIBSON

2 jiggers Vodka
½ jigger Dry Vermouth

Stir well with ice and strain
into glass. Serve with Pickled
Pearl Onion.

VODKA MARTINI

1 jigger Vodka
1/3 jigger Dry Vermouth

Stir with ice. Strain. Serve
with a twist of lemon peel.

VODKA SLING

1 jigger Vodka
½ jigger Cherry Brandy
Juice of ½ Lime

Fill highball glass half full
of ice. Place sliced cherries
around inside of glass. Add
lime and Vodka. Fill glass
with shaved ice. Add Brandy
Garnish with slice of orange,
cherry and peel of cucumber.
Do not stir or shake.

VODKA TWISTER

1 jigger Vodka
Lemon Soda
Juice of ½ Lime

Serve with ice in highball
glass. Add lime peel.

VODKA ABA SPECIAL

½ jigger Creme de Cacao
1 jigger Lemon Juice
4 jiggers Vodka

Shake with cracked ice.

VOLGA BOATMAN

1 jigger Vodka
1 jigger Cherry Brandy
1 jigger Orange Juice

Stir well with ice. Strain into
cocktail glass.

WAGON WHEEL

½ jigger Grenadine
1 jigger Lemon Juice
1½ jigger Cognac
4 jiggers Southern Comfort

Shake with cracked ice.

WALDORF STANDARD

1 jigger Bourbon Whiskey
1 jigger Pernod
1 jigger Sweet Vermouth
3 Dashes Angostura Bitters

Stir with ice and strain.

WALDORF COCKTAIL

1 jigger Whiskey
1 jigger Abisante or
   Anesone
1 jigger Sweet Vermouth
3 Dashes Bitters

Stir with ice and strain.

WALLICK'S SPECIAL

1 jigger Brandy
1 jigger Cream
1 Egg White
½ Teaspoon Powdered Sugar
2 Dashes Grenadine

Shake with ice and strain.

WALLICK'S

1 jigger Cherry Brandy
1 jigger White Curacao

Shake with ice and strain.

WARD STANDARD

1 jigger Whiskey
Juice of ½ Lemon
3 Dashes Grenadine

Shake with cracked ice and pour unstrained into tall glass. Fill with soda and decorate with cherry.

WASHINGTON

2 jiggers Dry Vermouth
1 jigger Brandy
2 Dashes Sugar Syrup
2 Dashes Angostura Bitters

Stir with ice and strain.

WEBSTER

2 jiggers English Gin
1 jigger Dry Vermouth
½ jigger Apricot Brandy
½ jigger Lime Juice

Shake with ice and strain.

WEDDING BELLE

1 jigger Dry Gin
1 jigger Dubonnet
½ jigger Orange Juice
½ jigger Cherry Brandy

Shake with ice and strain.

WEDDING MARCH

2 jiggers Light Rum
Juice of ½ Lime
2 Egg Whites
2 Dashes Angostura
   Bitters

Shake with ice and strain.

WEDDING NIGHT

3 jiggers Martinique Rum
½ jigger Maple Syrup
1 jigger Lime Juice

Shake with shaved ice and strain into Champagne glass.

WEEKENDER

1 jigger Dry Gin
1 jigger Curacao
1 jigger Dry Vermouth
1 jigger Sweet Vermouth
4 Dashes Pernod

Stir with ice and strain.

WELCOME STRANGER

1 jigger Dry Gin
1 jigger Swedish Punch
1 jigger Brandy
1 jigger Grenadine
1 jigger Lemon Juice
1 jigger Orange Juice

Shake with ice and strain.

WELLINGTON

1 jigger Dry Gin
2 Dashes Swedish Punch
2 Dashes Cherry Brandy
Juice of ½ Lime

Stir with ice and strain.

WEMBLEY NO. 1

2 jiggers Dry Gin
1 jigger Dry Vermouth
2-3 Dashes Calvados or
    Apple Brandy

Stir with ice and strain.

WEMBLEY NO. 2

1 jigger Scotch Whiskey
1 jigger Dry Vermouth
1 jigger Pineapple Juice

Shake with ice and strain.

WESTERN ROSE

1 jigger Dry Gin
½ jigger Dry Vermouth
½ jigger Apricot Brandy
1 Dash Lemon Juice

Stir with ice and strain.

WESTCHESTER ABA SPECIAL

1 jigger Lime Juice
1 jigger French Vermouth
4 jiggers Bourbon

Shake with cracked ice.

WEST INDIAN

2 jiggers Burrough's Beefeater
    Gin
4 Dashes Angostura Bitters
1 Teaspoon Sugar
1 Teaspoon Lemon Juice
2 Cubes Ice

Stir and serve.

WHISKEY STANDARD

1½ jiggers Bourbon Whiskey
2 Dashes Angostura Bitters
1 Dash Sugar Syrup

Stir with ice and strain.

WHISKEY 'N' BITTERS

1 jigger Whiskey
2 Dashes Bitters

Pour over ice cubes into over-
size whiskey glass. Stir well

WHISKEY COLLINS STANDARD

1 jigger Whiskey
Juice of ½ Lime

Stir with ice. Strain into
highball glass. Fill with soda
water.

WHISKEY FLIP

1 jigger Whiskey
1 Egg
1 Teaspoon Powdered Sugar

Shake w i t h cracked ice.
Strain. Sprinkle nutmeg on
top.

WHISKEY SOUR STANDARD

1 jigger Whiskey
Juice of ½ Lemon
½ Teaspoon Sugar

Shake well with ice. Strain
and garnish with cherry and
orange slice.

WHITE LION

1 jigger Dark Rum
Juice of ½ Lemon
1 Teaspoon Powdered Sugar
3 Dashes Bitters
3 Dashes Raspberry Sryup

Shake with ice and strain.

WHIZZ-DOODLE

1 jigger Dry Gin
1 jigger Creme de Cacao
1 jigger Scotch Whiskey
1 jigger Cream

Shake with ice and strain.

WHY NOT

1 jigger Dry Gin
1 jigger Dry Vermouth
2/3 jigger Apricot Brandy
1 Dash Lemon Juice

Shake with ice and strain.

WIDOW'S DREAM

2 jiggers Benedictine
1 Egg
1 jigger Cream

Shake with ice and strain.

WILD IRISH ROSE

1 jigger Irish Whiskey
½ Tablespoon Grenadine
Juice of ½ Lime

Shake w i t h cracked ice.
Strain and fill with chilled
soda water.

WILL ROGERS

1 jigger English Gin
½ jigger Dry Vermouth
½ jigger Orange Juice
4 Dashes Curacao

Shake with ice and strain.

WILSON STANDARD

2 jiggers Dry Gin
2 Dashes Dry Vermouth
2 Slices Orange

Shake with ice and strain.

WITCHING EVE

2 jiggers Creme de Cacao
1 Dash Angostura Bitters
1 jigger Cream

Pour carefully into glass do
not mix.

WILD OAT

3 jiggers Dry Gin
1 jigger Kirsch
1 Dash Lemon Juice
1 Dash Apricot Brandy

Shake with ice and strain.

WYOMING SWING

1 jigger Sweet Vermouth
1 jigger Dry Vermouth
1 Teaspoon Powdered Sugar
Juice of ¼ Orange

Shake with ice and strain.

X.Y.Z.

1 jigger Dark Rum
½ jigger Cointreau
½ jigger Lemon Juice

Shake with ice and strain.

XANTHIA

1 jigger Dry Gin
1 jigger Yellow Chartreuse
1 jigger Cherry Brandy

Stir with ice and strain.

XERES

2 jiggers Sherry
1 Dash Peach Bitters
1 Dash Orange Bitters

Stir with ice and strain.

YACHTING CLUB

2 jiggers Holland Gin
1 jigger Dry Vermouth
2 Dashes Sugar Syrup
2 Dashes Peychaud's Bitters
1 Dash Pernod

Stir with ice and strain.

YALE

1 jigger Gin
1/3 jigger Dry Vermouth
3 Dashes Orange Bitters
2 Dashes Sugar Syrup
1 Dash Maraschino

Stir with ice and strain.

YASHMAK

1 jigger Rye Whiskey
1 jigger Pernod
1 jigger Dry Vermouth
1 Dash Angostura Bitters
1 or 2 Pinches Sugar

Stir with ice and strain.

YELLOW PARROT

1 jigger Apricot Brandy
1 jigger Yellow Chartreuse
1 jigger Pernod

Shake with ice and strain.

YES AND NO

2 jiggers Brandy
4 Dashes Curacao
1 Egg White

Shake with ice and strain.

YO HO

1 jigger Rum
1 jigger Swedish Punch
1 jigger Calvados or Apple
   Brandy

Shake with ice and strain.
Serve with twist of Lemon
Peel.

YORK SPECIAL

3 jiggers Dry Vermouth
1 jigger Maraschino
4 Dashes Orange Bitters

Stir with ice and strain.

YOUNG MAN

3 jiggers Brandy
1 jigger Sweet Vermouth
2 Dashes Curacao
1 Dash Angostura Bitters

Stir with ice and strain.

ZHIVAGO STANDARD

1½ jiggers Vodka
½ jigger Kummel
Juice of ½ Lime

Stir with ice, strain into   a
champagne glass and serve
with an olive and a little
understanding.

ZAZARAC

1 jigger Rye Whiskey
½ jigger Sugar Syrup
½ jigger Anisette
½ jigger Light Rum
½ jigger Pernod
1 Dash Orange Bitters
1 Dash Angostura Bitters

Shake with ice and strain.
Squeeze Lemon Peel on top.

ZOOM

1½ jiggers Brandy
1/3 jigger Honey
½ jigger Cream

Shake with ice and strain.

ALL-AMERICAN NOG

½ Pint Bourbon
½ Pint Puerto Rican Rum
2 Quarts prepared dairy
   Eggnog
8 Small cups of ice cream

Stir eggnog mix and liquors in a large bowl. Remove ice cream from cups in one piece float on top of bowl. Scoop off a little ice cream to top each portion.

AMERICAN BEAUTY PUNCH

1 jigger White Creme de Menth
3 jiggers Orange Juice
2 jiggers Cognac
2 jiggers French Vermouth

Prepare and serve like Planters' Punch.

AMERICAN PUNCH

1 jigger Brandy
1 jigger Dry Vermouth
1 teaspoon Creme de
   Menthe
Juice of ½ Orange
½ Teaspoon Sugar

Shake with c r a c k e d ice. Strain into goblet filled with shaved ice and the Creme de Menthe.

APPLEJACK PUNCH

8 ounces Grenadine
1 pint Lemon Juice
1 pint Orange Juice
2 bottles Applejack
2 quarts Ginger Ale

Blend all the i n g r e d i e n t s other than the ginger ale and allow to ripen. Add ginger ale at time of serving.

ARTILLERY PUNCH

1 Quart Rye
1 Quart Claret
1 Quart Strong Black Tea
1 Pint Jamaica or Gold Label
   Rum
½ Pint Gin
½ Pint Cognac
1 jigger Benedictin
1 Pint Orange Juice
½ Pint Lemon Juice

Blend, allow to ripen, and pour over ice in Punch bowl.

B

BACCIO (Serves 8)

8 Oz. Calvert Gin
3 Oz. Anisette
8 Oz. Grapefruit Juice
Champagne

Combine in punch bowl over block of ice. Add sugar syrup to taste, orange slices, lemon slices. Before serving add 1 split chilled Champagne a n d 16 oz. chilled soda.

BALAKLAVA NECTAR

½ Pint Sugar Syrup
½ Pint Lemon Juice
Grate Peel of 3 or 4
    Lemons
2 Quarts Claret
3 Quarts Champagne

Mix ingredients other than champagne and a l l o w to ripen. Add champagne at time of serving.

BALTIMORE EGGNOG

Separate the W h i t e s and Yolks of 12 Eggs. Beat with the Egg Yolks 1 pound Powdered S u g a r. Stir in slowly 1 pint Brandy, ½ pint Light Rum, ½ pint Peach Brandy, 3 pints Milk and 1 pint Heavy Cream. Chill thoroughly and fold in stiffly beaten Egg W h i t e s before serving. Makes 25 to 30 cups.

96

BOMBAY PUNCH

2 Bottles Champagne
1 Pint Amontillado Sherry
1 Pint Brandy or Cognac
2 jiggers Curacao
2 jiggers Marachino Liqueur
2 Packages Frozen Sliced
    Peaches, half-thawed
1 Bottle Club Soda

Place sherry c o g n a c, Curacao, liqueur and peaches in bowl over block of ice. Stir. Chill in regrigerator. Before s e r v i n g add champagne and soda.

BUDDHA PUNCH (for 10)

¼ Quart Rhine Wine
4 jiggers Orange Juice
4 jiggers Lemon Juice
2 jiggers Curacao
2 jiggers Medium Rum
1 Dash Angostura Bitters

Combine in punch bowl with block of ice and just before serving add 1 bottle chilled Soda W a t e r and 1 bottle chilled Champagne. Garnish with twists of Lemon Peel and Mint leaves.

BURGUNDY PUNCH

Combine in punch bowl;
2 Bottles Burgundy
5 jiggers Port
3 jiggers Cherry Brandy
Juice of 3 lemons
Juice of 6 oranges
1 Tablespoon Sugar
1 long twist of Lemon and
   Orange Peel

Add block of ice. Before serving add 2 bottles chilled soda water.

BRANDY PUNCH OR RO-MAN PUNCH

1 jigger Raspberry Syrup
2 jiggers Lemon Juice
3 jiggers Cognac
1 jigger Jamaica Rum
2 or 3 Dashes Curacao to
   each drink

Prepare and serve like Planters' Punch.

BRIDE'S BOWL
(Serves 20)

1½ Quarts Leilani Rum
½ Pineapple, sliced
1 Pint Strawberries
¾ Cup Sugar Syrup
1 Cup Lemon Juice
2 Cups Pineapple Juice

Chill for 2 hours. Serve in punch bowl with block of ice, a d d i n g 1 pint thinly sliced s t r a w b e r r i e s and 2 quarts soda.

CARDINAL (1½ gallons)

Place 1½ pounds Sugar in a punch bowl and dissolve with 2 quarts Soda Water. Add 2 quarts Claret, 1 pint Brandy, 1 pint Rum, 1 jigger Sweet Vermouth, 1 sliced Orange and 3 slices Fresh Pineapple. Stir and add block of ice. Before serving add 1 pint of any Sparkling White Wine.

CEYLON (for 6)

3 jiggers Brandy
1½ jiggers Dry Vermouth
1 jigger Triple Sec
3 jiggers Dry Sherry
Juice of ½ Lemon
1 Stick of Cinnamon,
   Broken

Shake with ice and strain.

CHAMPAGNE CONTINEN—TAL PUNCH

Place 3 crushed pineapples in glass bowl. Cover with 1 pound of p o w d e r e d sugar and let stand 1 hour.

Add:
1 Pint Lemon Juice
2½ jiggers Maraschino
2½ jiggers Curacao
1 Pint Cognac
1 Pint Jamaica Rum

Stir. Cover and let stand 12-18 hours. Pour into punch bowl over large block of ice. Add 4 quarts champagne before serving.

CHAMPAGNE CUP

1 Bottle Iced Champagne
2 Ounces Benedictine
2 Ounces Gin
Juice of 1 Lime
2-3 Dashes Orange Bitters
1 Orange, cross section
   slices

Pour over cracked ice in a pitcher and stir briskly until cold. Strain into large pitcher or bowl. Add champagne and stir. Serve at once in cups or champagne glasses.

CHAMPAGNE PUNCH NO.1
   (1 gallon)

Combine in punch bowl ½ pound Powdered Sugar, 1 quart Soda Water, 2 jiggers Maraschino, 2 jiggers Curacao 3 jiggers Lemon Juice. Stir together and add block of ice. Pour in 2 or 3 bottles Champagne.

CHAMPAGNE PUNCH NO. 2
   (for 18)

Combine in the order named in a large punch bowl, with a block of ice, juice of 2 Lemons, 2 Oranges, ½ cup Sugar, ½ cup Light Rum, ½ Dark Rum, 1 cup Pineapple Juice. Stir lightly and pour in 2 b o t t l e s iced Champagne.

CHAMPAGNE PUNCH NO.3
   (for 20)

Place 1 quart either Lemon or Orange Ice in a punch bowl. Pour over it 2-3 bottles iced Champagne.

CHAMPAGNE PUNCH NO. 4 (for 15)

Place large block of ice in punch bowl. Add 2 jiggers Brandy, 2 jiggers Cointreau and 2 bottles iced Champagne.

CHAMPS ELYSEES (for 6)

6 jiggers Cognac
2 jiggers Yellow Chartreuse
2 jiggers Lemon Juice
1 Tablespoon Powdered Sugar
1 Dash Angostura Bitters

Shake with ice and strain.

CHARLES

½ jigger Brandy
½ jigger Sweet Vermouth
1 Dash Angostura or Orange Bitters

Stir with ice and strain.

CLARET CUP

½ Pint Sugar Syrup
½ Pint Lemon Juice
1 Pint Orange Juice
4 ounces Curacao
4 ounces Pineapple juice
2 ounces Maraschino
2 Quarts Claret
2 Quarts Club Soda

Add charged water only at time of serving.

CLARET PUNCH NO. 2

Mix together 2 bottles Claret, ¼ pound Sugar, the Rind of 1 Lemon and chill for several hours. Place block of ice in a punch bowl, pour in the iced mixture. Add 1½ jiggers Cognac, 1½ jiggers Curacao and 1½ jiggers Sherry. Before serving p o u r in 2 bottles chilled Soda Water. Makes 25 to 30 cups.

CHRISTMAS PUNCH NO. 2
(50 drinks)

In a large punch bowl combine 1 quart strong Tea with a bottle e a c h Rum, Rye Whiskey and Brandy, ½ bottle Benedictine, 1 tablespoon Angostura B i t t e r s and 1 sliced Pineapple. Add the Juice of 12 O r a n g e s, ½ pound Sugar, d i s s o l v e d in Water, and mix together thoroughly. Add block of ice before serving pour in 2 quarts of chilled Champagne.

COLONIAL TEA PUNCH

Remove the P e e l in thin strips from 12 Lemons and place the strips in a punch bowl. Add 1 quart strong Tea and the Juice from the Lemons. Mix with 2 cups Sugar and let stand for 1 hour. Add 1 quart Dark Rum and 1 jigger Brandy. Pour the mixture over crushed ice and serve. Makes 12 to 15 cups.

DRAGOON PUNCH

½ Pint Sugar Syrup
½ Pint Sherry
½ Pint Brandy
3 Pints Porter
3 Pints Ale
3 Pints Champagne
3 Lemons thinly sliced
Add Champagne just before serving.

FLAMINGO PUNCH

1 Bottle Champagne
1 Bottle Crackling Rose Wine
1 Container thawed whole
   frozen Raspberries

Place block of ice in punch bowl. Put in raspberries. Pour champagne and rose in simultaneously.

FESTIVAL PUNCH
(for about 10)

1 Quart Jamaica Rum
1 Quart Sweet Apple Cider
2 or 3 Sticks Cinnamon,
   broken
1 or 2 Tablespoons Butter

Heat ingredients in a heavy saucepan u n t i l almost boiling. Serve hot in mugs.

FISH HOUSE PUNCH NO. 1
(for 25)

Dissolve ¾ pound Sugar in a large punch bowl with a little Water. When entirely dissolved stir in 1 quart Lemon Juice, 2 quarts Jamaica Rum, 2 quarts Water and add Peach Brandy to taste. Place 1 large block of ice in punch bowl and allow mixture to chill 2 hours.

100

FISH HOUSE PUNCH NO. 2
(the best)

Dissolve in a punch bowl 1½ cups Sugar in 1 cup Water and 3 cups Lemon Juice. Add 3 pints Dry White Wine, 1 bottle Jamaica Rum, 1 bottle Gold Label Rum, 1 bottle Cognac and 2½ jiggers Peach Brandy. Let the mixture stand for 2 or 3 hours, stirring it occasionally. Before serving add a block of ice, stir to cool and serve.

GIN MINT PUNCH

1 jigger Sugar Syrup
2 jiggers Lemon Juice
3 jiggers Gin
1 or 2 sprigs Mint to each drink

Muddle the mint with the sugar and lemon juice and prepare like Planters' punch.

GIN PUNCH

2 bottles Gin
1 Pint Lemon Juice
1 Pint Cranberry Juice Cocktail
1 Quart Fresh Orange Juice
½ Cup Grenadine
2 ounces Orange Bitters

Pour over block of ice in a punch bowl. Stir and chill well. Add 1 quart club soda before serving. Garnish with sprigs of mint.

GIN PUNCH NO. 2
(for 12)

Combine juice of 12 lemons, 20 oranges, 2 quarts gin, 4 jiggers Grenadine. Pour over a large block of ice and add 2 bottles chilled soda water.

HUDSON BAY PUNCH

2 Bottles Canadian Whiskey
1 Can Frozen Orange Juice
1 Can Frozen Lemonade
1 Can Frozen Pineapple Juice
½ Pint Simple Syrup, or to taste
3 Quarts Strong Tea

Pour over block of ice in a punch bowl. Leave to chill. Decorate with any fruit.

LAFAYETTE PUNCH

Slice a half dozen oranges and arrange in bottom of Punch bowl. Sprinkle heavily with sugar, pour 1 bottle moselle wine over the fruit, and allow to stand 1 hour or more to ripen.   Place large block of ice in bowl and add 4 quarts champagne or 1 quart moselle and 3 quarts champagne at time of serving.

MAY WINE

Add 6 bunches of Waldmeister with ½ pound of powdered sugar.   Place in glass bowl and add ½ pint Cognac and 1 quart White Wine. Cover and let stand 12-18 hours. Stir, strain, and pour over ice into punch bowl. Before serving add 3 quarts White Wine and 2 quarts champagne.

MILK PUNCH (Basic)
(Serves 14)

1 Quart Calvert Extra
3 Quarts Milk
4 Oz. Powdered Sugar

Place in punch bowl over ice cubes. Beat well. Strain into mug or glass. Sprinkle with nutmeg.

NAVY PUNCH (for 10)

Slice 4 Pineapples and sprinkle well with 1 pound fine Sugar.   Add ½ bottle Dark Rum, ½ bottle Cognac, ½ bottle Peach Brandy and the Juice of 4 Lemons.   Chill well. Pour into punch bowl with block of ice. Decorate with fruit as desired and add 4 quarts of chilled Champagne.

NEW ORLEANS PUNCH

1 jigger Raspberry Sryup
2 jiggers Lemon Juice
1 jigger Jamaica Rum
2 jiggers Bourbon

Prepare like Planters' Punch except t h a t strong, cold, black tea is used in place of charged water.

PENDENNIS EGGNOG

Mix together 1 pound Powdered Sugar and 1 bottle Bourbon.   Let stand for 2 hours. Separate 12 Eggs and beat the Yolks to a froth, adding the Sweetened Whiskey slowly.   Let this stand for 2 hours. Whip 2 quarts Heavy Cream until stiff and whip the Egg Whites. Fold these s e p a r a t e l y into the Whiskey mixture and chill.

PICON PUNCH

1 jigger Grenadine
2 jiggers Lemon Juice
3 jiggers Amer Picon

Prepare and s e r v e like
Planters' Punch.

PINEAPPLE PUNCH (for 10)

1½ Quarts Moselle Wine
Juice of 3 Lemons
5 Dashes Angostura Bitters
2½ jiggers English Gin
2/3 jigger Pine Syrup
2/3 jigger Grenadine
2/3 jigger Maraschino

Pour all together into punch
bowl with 1 quart chilled
Soda Water. Set bowl in bed
of crushed ice to chill. Decorate with Pineapple.

PISCO PUNCH

In a large Wineglass or small
tumbler place 1 piece of ice
with a teaspoon each of Pineapple and Lemon Juice. Add
2 jiggers Brandy, a small cube
of Pineapple and fill with
cold Water

PITCHER PUNCH

1 Bottle Puerto Rican Gold
    Label Rum
1 Quart Pineapple Juice
1 Pint Cranberry Juice
    Cocktail

Mix well and chill. Pour off
as needed into a pitcher,
stir with ice. Garnish each
drink with a lemon wedge
and maraschino cherry.

PLANTATION PUNCH

Combine in a large Old-Fashioned glass 1 jigger Southern
Comfort, ½ j i g g e r Lemon
Juice, ½ Jigger Rum, 1 teaspoon Sugar. Fill with ice
and little Soda Water. Garnish with twist of Orange
Peel and serve.

PLANTER'S PUNCH

Using a tall glass with cracked
ice as desired, pour in 1 part
Lime Juice, 2 parts Sugar
Syrup, 3 parts Jamaica Rum,
4 parts Water. This may be
served w i t h a Maraschino
Cherry and a slice of Orange.
The ice and water should
be figured together as the
4 parts.

POOR MAN'S PUNCH

2 Quarts Red Bordeaux Wine
2 Quarts Club Soda
1 Pint Lemon Juice
½ Pint Simple Syrup
½ Pint Raspberry Syrup

Mix all except soda. Add soda before serving.

QUINTET

3 jiggers Brandy
3 jiggers dark Rum
4 Bottles White Wine
Juice of 8 Lemons
and 8 Oranges

Combine in bowl with block of ice. Before serving pour in 4 b o t t l e s chilled soda water.

REGENT PUNCH (for 10)

2½ jiggers Brandy
2½ jiggers Swedish Punch
1¼ jiggers Curacao
1 Pint Jamaica Rum
Juice of 6 Lemons
1 Cup Strong Tea
1 Teaspoon Angostura
  Bitters

1½ Quarts Champagne

Combine all the ingredients except the Champagne in a

punch bowl set in a bed of crushed ice. Just before serving, pour in the Champagne and garnish w i t h fruit as desired.

RHINE WINE PUNCH

3 Quarts Rhine Wine
1 Quart Chilled Soda Water
2½ jiggers Brandy
2½ jiggers Maraschino
1 Cup Strong Tea
½ Pound Powdered Sugar

Combine all the ingredients in a punch bowl set in a bed of crushed ice. Decorate with fruit as desired and serve when t h o r o u g h l y chilled. Makes 25 to 30 cups.

ROCKY MOUNTAIN PUNCH

4 Ounces Sugar Syrup
4 Ounces Maraschino
1 Pint Lemon Juice
1 Bottle Jamaica Rum
4 Quarts Champagne

Blend and ripen other ingredients and add champagne at time of serving.

ROMAN PUNCH (for 10)

2½ jiggers Brandy
2½ jiggers Swedish Punch
1¼ jiggers Curacao
1 Pint Jamaica Rum
Juice of 6 Lemons
1½ Quarts Chilled
   Champagne
1 Teaspoon Angostura or
   Orange Bitters
1 Cup Strong Tea

Combine all the ingredients in a punch bowl set in a bed of crushed ice. Garnish with fruit as desired and serve when thoroughly chilled. Framboise may be used instead of the Curacao.

RUM PUNCH

½ Pint Puerto Rican Rum
½ Pint Peach Brandy
½ Pint Lemon or Lime Juice
5 Tablespoons Bitters
6 Pints Soda Water

Stir rum, brandy, juice and bitters in a bowl. When ready to serve, add block of ice and soda.

RUM PUNCH GRANDE

10 Bottles White Wine
2 Pounds Brown Sugar
2 Quarts Orange Juice
1 Quart Lemon Juice
10 Sliced Bananas
2 Fresh Pineapples, cut or
   chopped

Place the Fruit Juice, Rinds, Bananas, Pineapple and Wine in a crock with the Sugar. Cover and let s t a n d overnight. In the morning add 6 bottles Light Rum and 1 bottle Jamaica Rum and 1 bottle Creme de Banane. Let stand until just before the party. Strain into punch bowl with ice as needed.

SCOTCH WHISKEY PUNCH
(Serves 12)

1 Quart Passport Scotch
Juice and Rind of 3 Lemons
½ Cup Sugar
1 Quart Soda

Combine in p i t c h e r with cracked ice. Pour into goblets with extra ice. Garnish with fruit slices.

VODKA BOMBAY PUNCH
(Serves 12)

1 Quart Vodka
1 Quart Sherry
¼ Pint Maraschino
½ Pint Curacao
2 Quarts Chilled Soda

Combine in a mixing bowl, without ice. Set punch bowl in bed of crushed ice. Decorate with fruits. Add 4 quarts c h i l l e d Champagne just before serving.

WHISKEY PUNCH

2 Quarts Blended Bourbon
3 Ounces Curacao
1 Quart Apple Juice
Juice of 6 Lemons
2 Ounces Grenadine
2 Large Bottles Iced Ginger Ale

Pour all but ginger ale over block of ice in punch bowl. Stir. Leave to chill. Add ginger ale before serving. Garnish with m a r a s c h i n o cherries.

XALAPA PUNCH

2½ Quarts Black Tea
1 Bottle Gold Label Rum
1 Bottle Claret
1 Bottle Applejack
1 Pint Sugar Syrup
1 Large Lemon Thinly sliced
Grated peel of 2 medium lemons

Pour the hot tea over lemon peels. After 15 minutes add the sugar syrup and stir. After cool, add the other liquids and pour over ice in bowl. Before s e r v i n g add lemon slices.

YACHT CLUB PUNCH

1 jigger Grenadine
2 jiggers Lemon Juice
3 jiggers Rum
2 or 3 Dashes Absinthe to each drink

Prepare and s e r v e like Planters' Punch.

STANDARD MEASURES

1 Gallon (U.S.)	128 ounces
½ Gallon	64 ounces
1 Quart	32 ounces
1 Fifth (4/5 Quart)	25.6 ounces
¾ Quart	24 ounces
1 Pint	16 ounces
1 Tenth	12.8 ounces
1 Cup (½ Pint)	8 ounces
1 Jigger	1½ ounces
1 Pony	1/8 ounce
1 Dash	3 Drops

STANDARD GLASSWARE

Cordial	1 ounce
Cocktail Glass	4 ounces
Jigger	1½ ounces
Old Fashioned Glass	4 ounces
Sour Glass	5 ounces
Champagne Glass	5 to 6 ounces
Collins Glass	12 ounces
Highball Glass	8 ounces
Julep Glass	10 to 12 ounces
Brandy Glass	3 ounces
Cordial Glass	2 ounces
Sherry Wine Glass	4 ounces
Standard Wine Glass	6 ounces